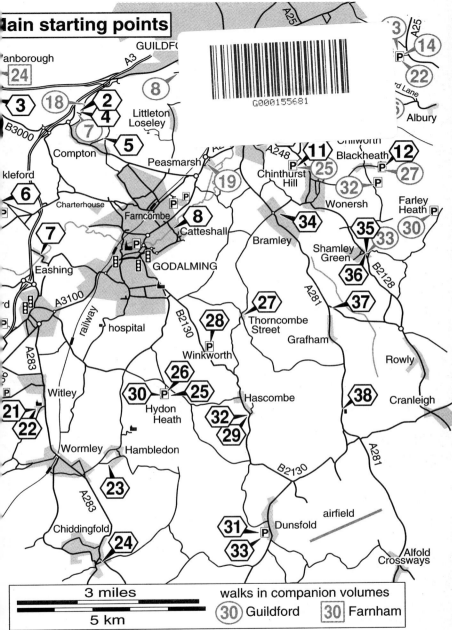

Main starting points

GUILDFORD

Farnborough 24

3 18 2 4

7 5

Littleton Loseley

8

Compton

Peasmarsh

19

A248 11 25

Chilworth

Blackheath 12

27

Chinthurst Hill

Albury

32

Wonersh

Farley Heath 30

kleford 6

Charterhouse

Farncombe

8

Catteshall

34

35 33

Bramley

Shamley Green

36

B2128

7

Eashing

GODALMING

A3100

railway

hospital

B2130

Grafham

27

Thorncombe Street

37

A281

Rowly

Witley

A283

28

Winkworth

26

25

Hascombe

38

Cranleigh

21 22

30

Hydon Heath

32 29

A281

Wormley

Hambledon

23

A283

B2130

airfield

Chiddingfold

24

31

Dunsfold

33

Alfold Crossways

3 miles

5 km

walks in companion volumes

30 Guildford   30 Farnham

The maps are reproduced from the Explorer Series (1:25 000) 145, 133 & 134 of 1997 by permission of Ordnance Survey on behalf of the Controller of Her Majesty's Stationery Office, © Crown Copyright MC 100011861.

Surrey Archæological Society gave permission for the drawings of the pot and arrowheads to be used. Haslemere Education Museum supplied the drawings.

1 Puttenham Common to the Hog's Back

About 6½ km/4 miles; good in winters; soft sand in summer. Puttenham Common is popular but confusing and best comprehended in small doses. OS maps: 1:25000 145 Guildford; 1:50000 186 Aldershot.

Linking walks 2❖ 3✧ 6✪ 13✦ 21❀ 22✳ 24❖

Start at Puttenham Common Top car park, SU 920 461 or Puttenham village (roadside parking), SU 930 478.

The Good Intent ☎ 01483 810387

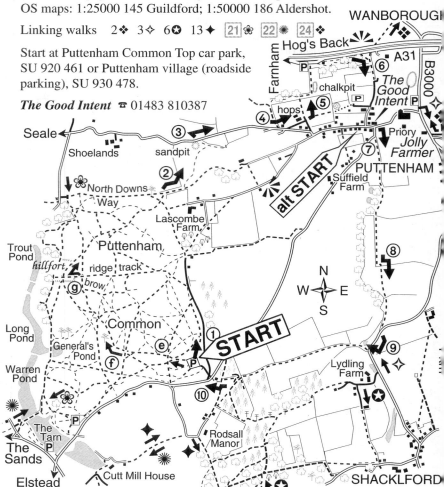

❀ If new to **Puttenham Common** start along the boundary track, ①. To cross part of the Common, start at ⓔ but allow time for confusion.

ⓔ *Drop down the steep path from the car park, diametrically opposite the access track (100m). Don't join the valley path but cross the slight rise and keep on to the next major junction, forking R when the path splits near the end (300m).*

ⓕ *Cross the sloping path and go over a rise, ahead and down past a 4-way junction (300m). After this disregard a L fork (50m) and go up over the brow of the hill (200m) to the ridge track beyond it (100m).*

ⓖ *Turn L through the ramparts of the hillfort (100m) then take the 1st side path back R down the hill-*

side, across the next descending path (200m) and into a dip (100m). Ignoring side paths, keep on up ahead to join a converging path (150m). Follow this into the deep dip then up over the perimeter path (300m) and on into the corner of the Common (80m). ✦②

① Join the east boundary track of Puttenham Common (on R) and follow it away from the road to the 2nd house. Carry on along the path. Don't turn R just after the house (800m) or at the footpath to Lascombe Farm (400m) but take the next R (100m) into the corner of the Common (70m).

② Join the **North Downs Way** out of the Common (100m). After the field L take the side path ½L undulating down the flank of the hill (overgrown by bracken, late summer) in Little Common (400m). Outside the next field turn L down the path to the lane below (50m).

③ Follow the lane R (600m).

④ After the 1st house L bear L on the track (Dark Lane) to the junction (150m).

⑤ Turn L to the farm sheds and go straight on up the middle of the hop field (150m). Climb the bank and turn R along the hillside (80m) then go up the L field boundary and through the trees to the Hog's Back car park (250m). Turn R. ❖

⑥ At the end of the car park keep on parallel with the road towards Guildford (300m) to the footpath down R (30m before the drive R). If traffic is light cross the dual carriageway from the drive to see the view then return and descend the path, which becomes a track then School Lane, to the village

street in **Puttenham** (500m). Turn L to the *Good Intent* (50m). ✧

⑦ Opposite the pub, start along Suffield Lane to the bend (70m). Near the gate of **Puttenham Priory** take the footpath ahead along the L edge of the field then between fields and on along the R edge of the next field (900m).

⑧ Just round the corner at the end cross into the next field and go straight over to the stile hidden under the L brow of the dip (200m). Descend the short steep hill and go on round R to the lane (250m).

⑨ Walk down the lane R (130m) ✪ and turn into the next field R. Follow the L boundary round to the large field (150m) then keep on ahead at the R edges of the fields up the slight valley (700m). After the last field stay on the path ahead past the wood ignoring side paths L & R (300m). ✦✳

⑩ At the end, drop to the sunken bridleway and, slightly L (10m), climb the path on the other side. Go past the garden fence to the road at Puttenham Common Top car park (150m).

The Puttenham hop field is the only remaining one in Surrey. The variety is *Fuggles* grown for the Hog's Back Brewery and other real ale producers. So far, it has not suffered verticillium wilt, a fungal disease which would end cultivation. A few of the plants are male (1:500) and look different. The oast houses below the church, now residential, functioned until 1970 and the hops are dried in the shed in the field. Hop growing came to the Farnham area just before 1600 and dominated agriculture on the malmstone in the 18th and 19th centuries.

2 Wanborough and the Hog's Back

8 km/5 miles; a scenic walk over fields, good all the year round; hilly, with many stiles and two perilous road crossings. OS maps: 1:25000 145 Guildford; 1:50000 186 Aldershot.

Linking walks 1❖ 3✳ 4✪ ⑤✳ ⑦★ ⑱✳ 23❖ 24✿

Start from Wanborough beside the Great Barn, SU 934 488, or from near Monks Hatch, SU 955 477, parking under the A3 on the North Downs Way off Down Lane near Watts Gallery, Compton.

Watts Gallery *Tea Shop* ☎ 01483 811030
Watts Gallery ☎ 01483 810235

✳① See **Wanborough Great Barn, Manor** house and church then follow the track past the church away from the road. Keep on between the fields (1100m) then round R & L bends and on along the drive to the junction at the East Flexford houses (500m).
② Go L down the cart track to the next junction (400m).
③ After a house, when the main track bends L, go R on the bridle-way between fields (450m) then out into a field. Horse riders often

confuse the way. Diverge from the L hedge to a path junction at the protruding hedge bend (250m).
④ Take the track R which goes across the middle of the field up to trees (200m) then along the field boundaries (300m). ★ Cross the track at the corner of Chalkpit Wood and continue on the path to the houses then straight up the

4

gravel drive to the top of the **Hog's Back** (500m).

⑤ Cross the dual carriageway and go slightly R (30m) to find a path into the field on the other side. Go straight down, over a cart track and across a terrace then down to the tarmac lane (200m). Keep on ahead down the field parallel with the R fence. In the 2nd field follow the bottom boundary down past a knoll with trees (300m). Cross the end of a 3rd field then turn R beside the road embankment to the gateway of **Monks' Hatch** (200m). ✻✿♻✻ The alternative parking area is L through the A3 bridge.

⑥ Turn R along the **North Downs Way**. A cart track joins from the R (600m). Carry on ahead to the next group of houses (200m). ❖

⑦ After the 1st house (50m) turn R at the drive of Monks Grove Farm. Pass between the gardens and go straight up the slope, over the golf course and through belts of trees (300m). At the top of the wood bear L behind the tee (100m) to the farm track. Go over the field to the furthest corner (100m) and cross the track into the next field. Keep on up the R edges onto the Hog's Back (400m).

⑧ Cross the dual carriageway and, slightly L (30m), descend the footpath (old carriage road) to **Wanborough** (800m). ✻

The Hog's Back is the most contorted part of the North Downs chalk ridge. It was once part of a dome over the Weald but the middle has been eaten out by erosion to leave this broken edge; the South Downs are the other edge. To the north the chalk dips under London to re-surface as the Chilterns beyond.

The field track from Wanborough runs along the edge of the London Clay on which grow cereals. Water out of the chalk overflows the edge of the clay and the springs were the likely attraction for the original settlers. The wooded hills visible to the north are the escarpment of the Tertiary (Bagshot) Sands plateau with infertile heath stretching to Bracknell. It resists erosion because of a cap of flint gravel washed out from the chalk dome by the early Ice Age torrents.

Melbourne Rock, a layer in the Middle Chalk, was quarried at Puttenham and used in the pillars of Compton Church. The Upper Greensand under the Chalk permits the hops to grow at Puttenham and yields the white malmstone seen in the village. Gault clay accounts for the Puttenham valley as it allows the edge of the chalk to be undermined by erosion; it provided the raw material for the terracotta of the Watts chapel. The Folkstone Beds, top stratum of the Lower Greensand, are unlithified sands lacking calcium; they are responsible for the heathland of Puttenham golf course and Common. The calcareous Bargate sandstone outcrops as the plateau above Compton. This stretches to Hascombe interrupted by the gorges of the Rivers Wey and Ock at Godalming, quarried for the excellent brown stone seen in old walls in the area. The escarpment is scalloped into the coombs which have found their way into village names.

3 Puttenham and Shackleford

9 km/5½ miles with a bluebell extension of 1 km/¾ miles through Compton; good all the year round with plenty to see; mostly across fields; one short steep hill; many stiles, one nasty road crossing and the hazards of golf.
OS maps: 1:25000 145 Guildford; 1:50000 186 Aldershot.

Linking walks   1✧ 2✳ 4✿ 5✿ 6★ ⑱✪ 23✸ 24✳

Start at the parking layby on the B3000 at the Puttenham turn, SU 934 479 or at Shackleford car park, SU 935 453.

The Cyder House ☎ 01483 810360
The Good Intent ☎ 01483 810387
The Harrow Inn ☎ 01483 810379
The Jolly Farmer ☎ 01483 810374

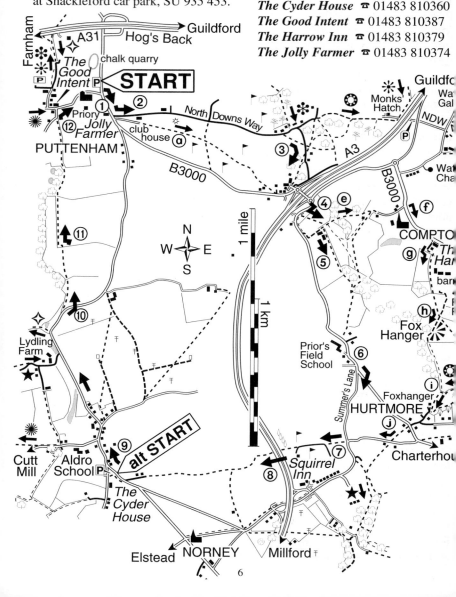

6

① Walk down the B3000 to the ***Jolly Farmer*** (100m) and cross the road to the rough track L (the **North Downs Way**).

ⓐ *Alternative: Follow the right-of-way along the golf course.*

② Follow the NDW past Clear Barn (400m) and a side track L (300m), to houses L (500m). ☻

③ Opposite Monksgrove Cottage join the path R diagonally over the golf course into the wood, ignoring golf tracks R & L (150m). On the vehicle track turn R to the first house (50m) then fork R and carry on to the road (300m). Cross the A3 junction bridge (150m) and go R (towards Charterhouse) (150m).

④ At the bend, opposite the first drive, go L up the fields aiming L of the sheds (250m).

ⓔ *Extension of 1 km/¾ mile via* **Compton**: *At the sheds turn L and go down the path and on along the lane to the main road (600m).*

ⓕ *Walk down the village street R to the* **Harrow** *(300m).*

ⓖ *Go down the drive beside the pub (70m) and L behind gardens (50m) then up the R boundary of the field over the rise (200m) and straight across the next field in the same line to the cart track (200m).*

ⓗ *Follow it up R over the spur of the hill and down to the corner (200m) and continue up round the boundary of the next field (300m).*

ⓘ *Just before the next corner exit R and take the uphill path (150m). Go straight on along the track, over the main road (150m) and along the track opposite (150m).* ★

ⓙ *Turn R on the road to the bend at Summer's Lane (300m).* ➔⑦

⑤ Carry on ahead on the path next to the shed and along the edge of the field above the bargate escarpment to the road near **Prior's Field School** (900m).

⑥ Walk along the road L (250m) then R down Summer's Lane to the road junction (500m). ★

⑦ From the junction go across the golf links in a straight line (faint path then vehicle track then invisible path) to the exit at L end of a line of conifers (500m).

⑧ Cross the dual carriageway and go along the track opposite (1000m). (Ignore a side track L, 250m after L bend.) At the end, cross the road and follow the path above it R to a Y-junction (150m). The ***Cyder House*** is L (100m). ✳

⑨ Walk on through **Shackleford**, past roads L & R (300m) and out of the hamlet. Ignore the lane L to Lydling Farm at the roadside pond (550m) and keep on. Don't turn off at the path in the field L at the next bend ◇ (150m) but join the path in the next field L (130m).

⑩ Follow the L edge of the field up the short steep slope under trees into the 2nd field (250m). Climb onto the brow and cross slightly R to enter the next field near the raised corner (200m).

⑪ Go round the corner of the field and on along the L boundary, through a wooded part then along the R boundary to the lane in **Puttenham** (900m) next to the gate of **Puttenham Priory** R . Carry on a few steps to the end of Suffield Lane opposite the ***Good Intent*** (70m). ✳✳

⑫ Turn R, and follow the road past **Puttenham Church** up to the main road and car park (400m).

4 Compton and Binscombe

About 7½ km/4¾ miles; good all the year round; mainly across farming country. OS maps: 1:25000 145 Guildford; 1:50000 186 Aldershot.

Linking walks   2❂   3❂   5❈   ⑦ ❈   ⑱ ♣   24 ✿

Start from Monks' Hatch, Compton, SU 955 477; park under the A3 beside the North Downs Way, off Down Lane near Watts Gallery.

The Harrow Inn ☎ 01483 810379   Watts Gallery ***Tea Shop*** ☎ 01483 811030
The Withies ☎ 01483 421158   Guildford

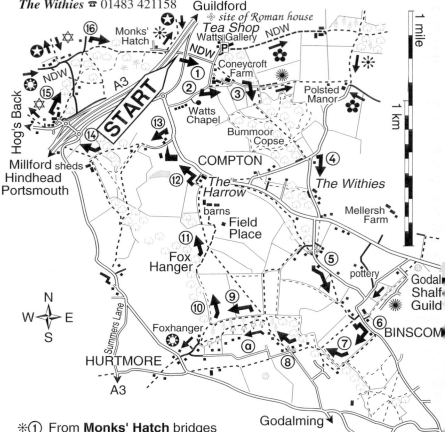

❈① From **Monks' Hatch** bridges follow the tarmac **North Downs Way** to the lane (400m). ♣ (**Watts Gallery** & ***Tea Shop*** are L 100m) then go R to the end of Coneycroft Farm buildings (200m).
If visiting **Watts Chapel** *carry on along the lane (200m) and into the cemetery then return.*

② Take the path L which zigzags beside the barns and continue on the straight farm track (400m). ❈
③ At the end boundary take the path R which skirts the field into the wood (200m) and carry on to the lane (500m).

8

④ Slightly L (10m) continue on the lane ahead past the **Withies** (200m) to the end (200m). Cross the main road and keep on along the grass to join the parallel lane when it bends L (250m). Carry on along the lane (150m).

⑤ Turn into the 2nd field R and cross diagonally to the top L corner (200m). Carry on behind the houses (150m).

⑥ At the end turn L (50m) into **Binscombe**. Follow the road R past the Quakers' burial ground and on (150m) then walk up the R edge of the 1st field R (300m).

⑦ At the top take the path round the top of the adjoining field R either in the field or through the trees above it (250m). From the next corner climb the stepped path up the side of the scarp and pass between gardens (200m).

⑧ At the road bend turn R along another path between gardens and keep on to the edge of the escarpment (300m).

ⓐ *Bluebell alternative: Turn L up through the coppice above the escarpment to the end of the path (500m) and double back down the path below the house, Foxhanger, into the field (200m)* ➔ ⑩

⑨ Descend the stepped path into the coomb (100m). Turn L on the path between the escarpment and the field (350m). After the R bend (20m) don't stay on the main path up L but enter the field.

⑩ Follow the boundary path round the top of the field (300m). Carry on up the curving track in the 2nd field to the top of the rise (100m) then start descending towards the large house, Field Place (100m).

⑪ Halfway down enter the field L and cross diagonally to the L of the distant barns (200m). In the next field follow the L edge over the rise and down past the barns (200m). Turn L behind the garden (50m) and R to the **Harrow** (70m).

⑫ Walk up the village street through **Compton**, past White Hart Cottage and Eastbury Manor. Visit the church then carry on up the road (300m).

⑬ Turn L along Eastbury Lane. At the end (250m) either take the hill path straight up (350m) or turn L on the other path then go up the fields R to rejoin the path on top.

⑭ Just before the sheds on top find the path R down through the middle of the fields to the bend in the road (200m). Go R on the road and over the A3 interchange bridge (300m). ✿

⑮ Continue ahead to the garage (50m) then take the path R into the wood. ✪ Near the houses R (300m) cross the cart track obliquely and a path and keep on down to the 4-way junction at the North Downs Way (250m).

⑯ Turn R along the NDW and stay on it to the Monks' Hatch bridges (600m).

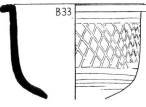

B33

Romano-British pot, probably 2nd century, found with many other shards on ground disturbed when the Binscombe Cresent houses were built in 1953. Archæologist's sketch showing section as well as surface. x¼ SAC <u>57</u> 1960 *Romano-British Farms*

5 Binscombe and Loseley

About 8 km/5 miles; good all the year round; mostly across farming country;
bluebell woods. In summer Loseley House can be visited *en route*.
OS maps: 1:25000 145 Guildford; 1:50000 186 Aldershot.

Linking walks   3✪   4✳   ⑦✤   ⑱✳   ⑲✧   24✳

Start from Compton. Park on the verge opposite *The Withies*, SU 963 468.

The Harrow Inn ☎ 01483 810379   **The Withies** ☎ 01483 421158
Watts Gallery *Tea Shop* ☎ 01483 811030   **Watts Gallery** ☎ 01483 810235
                    Loseley House ☎ 01483 304440

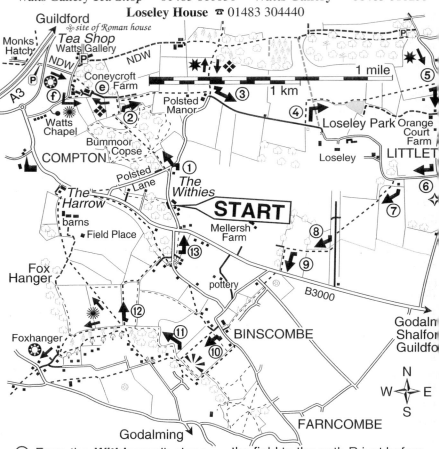

① From the **Withies** walk along
the lane away from the main road
(200m). Slightly L at the junction
with Polsted Lane take the path
between field and wood. Ignore all
side paths. At the end of the wood
(500m) skirt round the R edge of

the field to the path R just before
the concrete farm track (200m). ✤
ⓔ *If visiting* **Watts Gallery** *and/or*
***Tea Shop**: Go L on the concrete
farm track (200m), R on the footpath at the start of the buildings
(150m) and R on the lane (100m).*

Return along the lane to the end of the farm buildings (200m) then

ⓕ *go L on the path which zigzags beside the barns and on to the end of the farm track (400m).*

② Follow the footpath outside the boundary of the hillside field, ultimately past a garden and down into the sunken track (600m). ✳

③ Go out to the lane R in front of Little **Polstead** (10m) then turn L and follow the cart track past a house (400m) and on to the edge of **Loseley** Park (300m).

④ Take the path L just before the buildings and follow it away from the track (300m), round R, across another farm track and along the R field boundary past the pond (400m), (**Loseley House** visible far R) then straight on over the fields, out to the lane at Pillar Box Cottage in **Littleton** (500m).✧

⑤ Turn R along the lane through the village (600m).

⑥ Go R on the Loseley drive as far as the 1st house L (300m).

⑦ Next to the house drive take the track L into the field (50m) and cross the R corner (100m) to the next field. After a few steps beside the ditch continue diagonally. Aim for the bottom R corner (400m).

⑧ Before the corner join the cart track between the fields and go L to the ditch (100m). Cross it and follow it R through the fields. When the ditch bends R keep on ahead to the next hedge (350m).

⑨ Follow the hedge L to the road (200m). Slightly R (30m) cross into the football field opposite and go over it parallel with the R end (100m). Cross the next road to the grass, slightly L, and follow the R

fences parallel with the road to emerge in **Binscombe** next to the Quakers' cemetery (450m).

⑩ On the lane go R (40m) then L on the track between the houses (50m). When it bends go straight on up the field (250m). Look back.

> The Hog's Back is the hill L. Beyond the cluster of radio masts is Guildford at the notch where the River Wey cuts the chalk ridge. On the highest point Semaphore House gleams in the sun. The North Downs disappear behind Chantries Hill with St Martha's as the bump on the R end. The sharp green spire in front of Chantries is Shalford Church. The river runs between it and the Mount Browne Surrey Police HQ at the lone radio mast slightly L. The large house just beyond Binscombe is Loseley. The distant eminence R is the Leith Hill range. The closer Farley Hill and the plateau behind you are capped by Bargate sandstone and form the portals of the Wey gorge.

⑪ Join the path outside the field and turn R. Don't climb the scarp but branch R almost immediately on the winding path inside the edge of the wood (250m). At the gulley descend briefly (40m) then climb the L bank. Ignore paths in the fields below and keep on to the end of the wood at the path junction below steps (200m). ✳⊙

⑫ Go down the path between the fields (300m). Cross the ditch into the field below and turn R. Follow the R edges round down to the end of the fields (300m) then turn R along the track under the trees to the road (50m).

⑬ Cross to the grass and walk L parallel with the road (200m). Keep on over the main road along the lane to the *Withies* (200m).

6 Eashing, Peper Harow and Shackleford

About 8 km/5 miles, with an extension of 1km/½ mile; through fields and woods with a dash across the A3; soft sand and nettles in summer, little shade, gentle rises. OS maps: 1:25000 145 Guildford; 1:50000 186 Aldershot.

Linking walks   1✳   3★   7✦   13❀   26 ✳

Start from Shackleford car park, SU 935 453, or from Lower Eashing, at the west end of the bridges, SU 946 438.

The Stag ☎ 01483 421568
The Cyder House ☎ 01483 810360

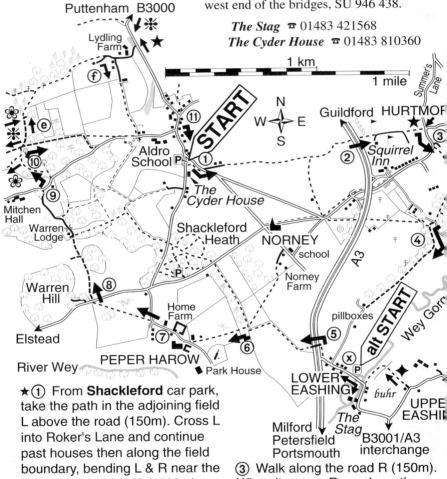

★① From **Shackleford** car park, take the path in the adjoining field L above the road (150m). Cross L into Roker's Lane and continue past houses then along the field boundary, bending L & R near the end, to the road (A3) (1100m).

② Cross the dual carriageway and keep on in the same line right across the golf course: on grass then cart track until it bends, then footpath to the houses. Emerge at a road bend in **Hurtmore** (500m).

③ Walk along the road R (150m). When it curves R, go down the footpath L, beside a drive. Ignore the uphill side paths and continue down to a cart track and garden wall in the Wey gorge (600m). ✦

④ Go R a few steps on the track then turn off L, up the bridleway

12

on the valleyside. Disregard the path up R into the trees. Continue on the level bridleway to the **pillboxes** then on the concrete farm track into **Eashing** (1200m).

ⓧ *Extra to see the village: Go L to Eashing Bridges (250m) and on to The Stag (150m), then return.*

⑤ Walk out of the village to the the A3 (100m). Turn R up over the bridge into the field (150m) then follow the R edge round to the 2nd corner at the trees (500m).

⑥ Join the track out of the field but immediately turn L through the trees (40m). In the next field go straight on parallel with the bottom boundary and L of the dovecote and barn, to **Peper Harow** Church (350m). **Park House** is visible L beyond the cricket field.

⑦ From the church walk up the lane (50m). Step into the yard R to see Home Farm then carry on up the lane (250m). When it bends R, go on into the field and diagonally up R to the far top corner (400m).

⑧ Cross the road into the field. Follow the track to Warren Lodge (450m) and straight on (450m).

⑨ At the road go R (100m) then turn L up the path into the wood round the end of the field (300m). ✾ Join another path up R to the 4-way junction (70m). ✳

ⓔ *Extension: Take the track ahead, between the wood and fields all the way to Lydling Farm house L (1100m).*

ⓕ *Backtrack (30m) and take the side turn past Lydling Cottages to the end (150m). Carry straight on along the bottom edge of the field to the road (400m) and follow it L to Shackleford (250m).* ↯⑪

⑩ Take the track R through the wood to the bend (400m) then go down the field ahead converging on the R edge to the bend (200m). Drop to the road and carry on to the end in Shackleford (400m).

⑪ Turn R to the car park (200m). the *Cyder House* is along the R fork (100m).

Charterhouse School has spires which make it a distinctive landmark on many of the walks in this book though there is no public path or road which allows a close view. It is one of the best known public schools, with 700 boys and 6th form girls. The name comes from its first position near Barts in London where a Carthusian monastery had stood. Thomas Sutton bought the post-Dissolution site from the Duke of Norfolk in 1611 and founded the school. It removed to Godalming after the main building was completed in 1872. *Photo Adrian Furniss*

7 Eashing, the River Wey and Godalming

About 8 km/5 miles or 1½ km/1 mile less if bypassing Godalming town centre; good views in winter, few stiles, one steep slope, little mud, quite a lot of tarmac. OS maps: 1:25000 145 Guildford; 1:50000 186 Aldershot.

Linking walks 6✦ 8✳

Start from Lower Eashing; park on the verge at the west end of the bridges, SU 946 438. If starting at Godalming, park at the kerbside in Borough Road or Peperharow Road or in one of the town centre car parks.

The Red Lion ☎ 01483 415207   ***The Stag*** ☎ 01483 421568

✦① From Eashing bridges walk through Lower **Eashing** towards the main road (200m). Before the last house R, turn into the tarmac drive and go on along a concrete farm track (400m). After the **pillboxes** continue ahead on the bridleway round L into a side valley where a drive and path join L on the two sides of the garden wall (900m).

ⓐ *When leaves are off the trees try taking the higher path: Go L on the side path after the wall (60m) then R up the valley side (100m). Near the top go R on the path along the steep side of the gorge (800m). Butchers broom abounds.*

ⓑ *After turning into the next side valley, go down the stepped side path R, and out down the tarmac Charterhouse drive to Peperharow Road (250m) into the footpath opposite.* ✦③

② Follow the track round the end of the valley to a house and keep to the path through the Wey gorge to Peperharow Road in **Godalming** (800m).

③ Walk down the path beside the houses to the river (100m) then follow the path L along the bank (450m). Join the tarmac path and stay on it to Borough Road (700m).

Just before the end, it crosses the drive to offices on the site of the old **Westbrook Mill.**

④ Pass under the railway bridge. and along the path behind the wall over the river (200m). Short route: turn R along Vicarage Walk. ✦⑧ Longer route: turn L into the public gardens at the **Phillips Memorial** cloisters then follow the riverside path to the next road (700m). ✳

⑤ Cross the bridge and double back R around the wall. Follow the river bank till you see Godalming Wharf (which was the end of the **Godalming Navigation**) (300m). Return to the bridge and cross it.

⑥ Walk up Bridge Street and on along High Street to the Pepperpot, the building on pillars (600m). (The **Red Lion** is 50m further on).

⑦ Walk down Church Street to **Godalming Church** (200m) then R along Borough Road (100m) and L into Vicarage Walk (100m).

⑧ Follow the lane R under the railway and up past **Westbrook House** to the top of the hill (600m).

⑨ When the lane bends L as a private drive to Westaway, go straight on along the gravelled drive past Shepherd Cottage (private drive but public footpath). After it, disregard the track L and continue ahead on the broad track past flat fields between the Ock and Wey gorges (spires back R are Charterhouse School) (900m).

⑩ At the end go R along the road (250m), round the L bend at Upper Eashing and on (250m).

⑪ At the first house R turn into the track and walk straight across the field along the shoulder (edge of the **burh**) to the stile just over the brow (250m). Descend L through the trees on the river bank to Eashing Bridges (200m). The **Stag** is ahead (100m).

Charterhouse Hog's Back A3/B3000

Peperharow Road

alt START

Wey Gorge

Guildford

Westbrook ⑧

④ ⑤

⑦ P P P ⑥

High Street

wharf

Red Lion

GODALMING

B2130

railway River Ock A3100

Winkworth Hascombe

ford / mill Tuesley

Escingum **burh** is recorded in the "Burhal Hidage", written around 915. Burhs became boroughs. They were 27 barracks set up in Wessex to counter Viking predations. Probably initiated by Alfred the Great, they provided a standing army which drove the Danes out of Wessex. For manning and sustenance they were apportioned parts of the kingdom. The 600 hides allocated to Escingum indicate a garrison of 600 men. Four defenders were stipulated for each pole (5½ yards) of wall and the figures accord with the square of land at Eashing between the river cliff and two dry side valleys (where the road and footpath lie) if the cliff was unmanned. Adjacent burhs were at Southwark, Winchester, Chichester and Sashes Island (at Cookham). Why Eshing lost its importance is obscure but many burhs became new towns as the influx of defenders required markets and services. More burhs were added in Mercia when the non-Danish parts were absorbed by Alfred's son and they were copied by the Franks.

8 Catteshall and Unsted

About 7½ km/4½ miles with an extension of 3½ km/2 miles. Good all the year but best when the Navigation is active; hilly; soft sand on the towpath in summer. OS maps: 1:25000 145 Guildford; 1:50000 186 Aldershot.

Start at from the bridge in Catteshall Road, SU 981 445 (kerbside parking). On the extension use the car park at the east end of Broad Water, SU 985 453.

Linking walks   7✳   9✳   27☆

Hector's on the Wey at Farncombe Boat House ☎ 01483 418769
The Manor Inn ☎ 01483 427134

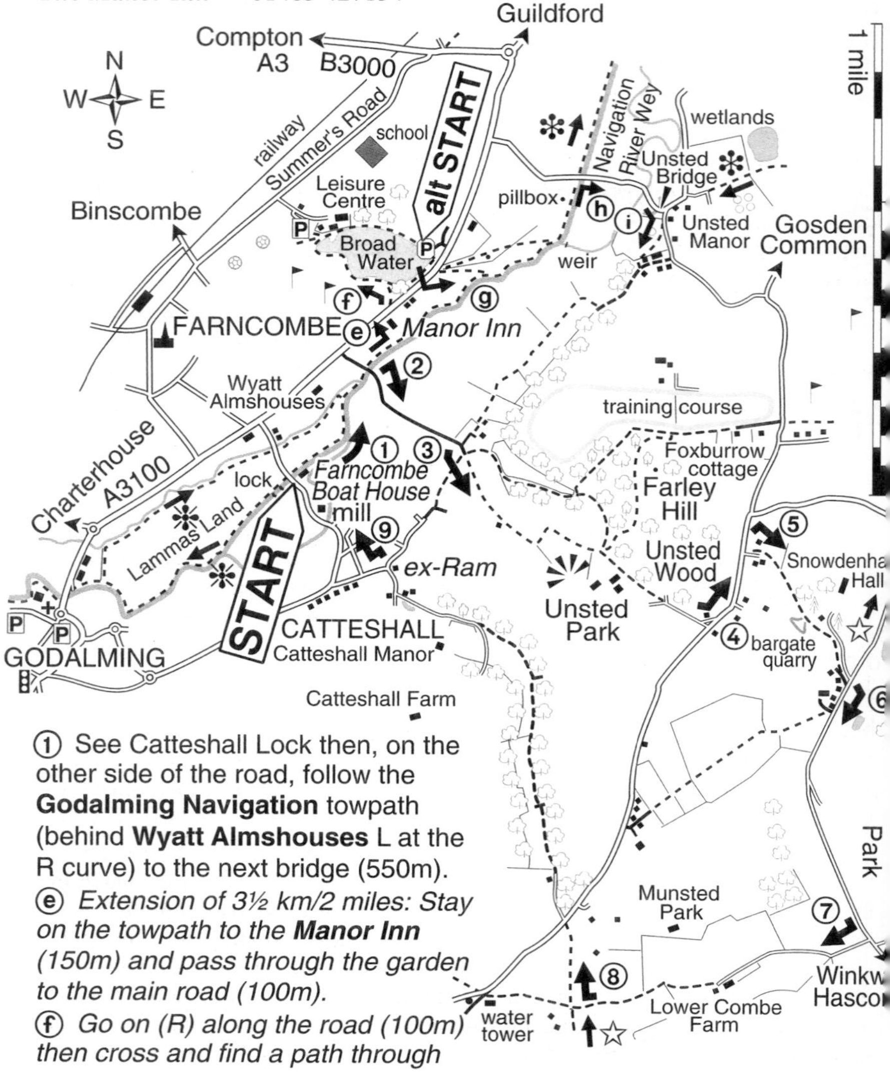

① See Catteshall Lock then, on the other side of the road, follow the **Godalming Navigation** towpath (behind **Wyatt Almshouses** L at the R curve) to the next bridge (550m).

ⓔ *Extension of 3½ km/2 miles: Stay on the towpath to the **Manor Inn** (150m) and pass through the garden to the main road (100m).*

ⓕ *Go on (R) along the road (100m) then cross and find a path through*

16

the trees to Broad Water pond. Walk round the pond L to the car park near the main road (700m).

(g) *From the east corner of the pond cross the main road to the field (50m) and take the footpath ahead (250m) then the towpath L to the bridge (500m).* ✳

(h) *Follow the lane over the canal, the river and, at the bend, the ancient* **Unsted Bridge** *(350m).*

(i) *Turn into Unsted Lane (20m) then cross the field R to the corner beyond the barn (150m). Exit via the path to the track near houses (30m) and go R over a rise and down (250m). At the end of the track turn R then L on the fenced path along the fields to a house (550m). Walk out along the drive (150m) then L.* →③

② Cross the Navigation and follow the track past the drive of the next house L (400m).

③ At the 4-way junction continue straight up the valleyside with views of the Wey valley behind and **Unsted Park** ahead (950m). Over the top follow the tarmac drive down to the road (150m).

④ Go L on the road and start down the hill (300m).

⑤ Enter the drive to the house Wood End and take the footpath L of the garden. Carry on under trees to the next road at Orchard Cottage (600m). ☆

⑥ Follow the road R (1000m).

⑦ Take the tarmac drive R up to Lower Combe Farm (550m) and continue past the buildings on the track then up the bridleway under trees (550m).

⑧ At the 4-way junction take the footpath down R between fences to the road (300m). Cross into the drive opposite. Walk down to the house and on into the valley past the gates of Catteshall Farm (1200m) and **Catteshall Manor** to the bottom (400m).

⑨ Turn L along Catteshall Lane (80m) ✳ then R along Catteshall Road (120m). Walk through the housing estate and on along the main road past **Catteshall Mill** to the bridge at Farncombe Boat House (300m).

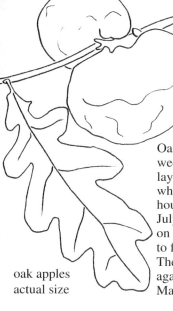

oak apples
actual size

Oak apples are green outgrowths that form in two weeks in May. A 4 mm wasp, *Biorhiza pallida*, lays its eggs in a bud. They release pheromones which re-program the bud to grow into the gall, housing about 30 grubs. The new wasps hatch in July, mate and crawl downwards to lay their eggs on the roots. These induce small, hard root galls to form for over-wintering with one grub each. The next generation wasps lay their eggs in buds again, without fertilization. Oak Apple Day, 29th May, marks the restoration of Charles II in 1660.

9 Shalford, Gosden Common and Unstead

About 6 km/3¾ miles but hilly extensions of 1 km/¾ mile and 3km/2 miles can be added. Good wetland birdwatching in winter. Fairly shady.
OS maps: 1:25000 145 Guildford; 1:50000 186 Aldershot.

Start from the green in Shalford, TQ 002 469, or *The Parrot* or Chinthurst Hill car park, TQ 014 463. Shalford station is near the route.

Linking walks   8❋   10★   11✧   34✿   ⑲✺   ⑳❋   ㉕✾

The Parrot ☎ 01483 561400   *The Queen Victoria* ☎ 01483 561733

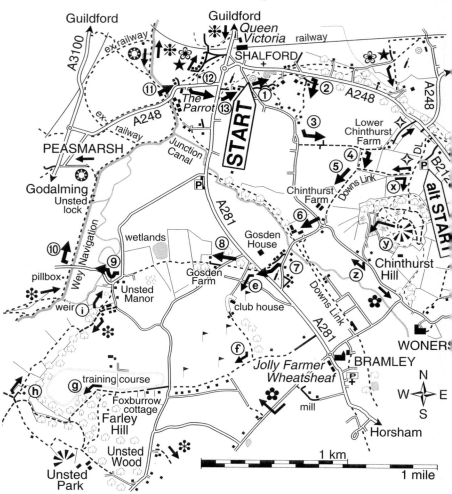

★❋ ① Starting from Chinthurst Lane in **Shalford** green, go over the grass to skirt the edge of the pond (surrounded by bushes) (200m). Carry straight on into the corner of the green (200m).

18

② After Station Road L and Ashley House R pass one more house then turn R on the path between houses to the next lane (250m) and follow it L (200m).

③ At the end of the 1st field L turn off L on the path between the fields (450m). ✧

④ Just over the rise and round the curve enter the field R and cross to the track (150m).

✿ⓧ *An extra 1km/¾ miles over* **Chinthurst Hill***: Take the track L (400m) then upward paths to the tower on top (400m).*

ⓨ *Behind the tower (opposite the doorway) descend by the steepest path (200m) and go on down the tarmac drive (350m) to the lane.* ✿

ⓩ *Walk down the lane R to the next junction (500m). Turn L.* ➜⑥

⑤ Keep on ahead on the track down to the lane junction (500m)

⑥ Go on down the side lane over the old **Horsham Railway** (course of the Downs Link path) and **Cranleigh Water** bridges (300m).

⑦ At **Gosden** Common turn off the lane along the R edge of the cricket green (250m). Cross the main road and follow the path, opposite, to a tarmac drive (100m).

ⓔ *Extension of 3km/2miles: Go L up the golf club drive, straight up through the sloping car park (350m), between huts and ahead along the right of way which skirts the brow of the hill (400m).*

ⓕ *At the far side turn R along the boundary, on the path outside or over the grass inside, to the lane (600m). Cross and continue along the drive past Foxburrow Cottage (150m) then the bridleway beside the wood (200m).*

ⓖ *Disregard the footpath L and go on round L into the wood down to a T-junction (450m). Descend R into the Wey valley (400m).*

ⓗ *At the bottom turn R along the drive past the house (100m) and, L of the stables, keep on along the fenced path (600m). After R & L bends (100m) follow the farm track over the rise (200m).*

ⓘ *At the next house take the side path L (30m) and go straight over the field towards the L-most house (100m).* ❊ *Join the lane and go L (40m) and L again.* ➜⑨

⑧ Carry on ahead over a lane (200m) along Gosden Farm drive (100m) then between fields (**wetlands** R) and out past the sewage works to the lane near **Unsted Manor** (500m). Go L along the lane ❊ (100m) and round the bend.

⑨ Follow the lane across the Wey Valley, over **Unsted bridge** (above a backwater), the River Wey Bridge and the **Godalming Navigation** Bridge (400m).

⑩ Descend to the towpath R and follow it past Unsted Lock (500m), the Peasmarsh path L ✪ (100m), the old Horsham Railway bridge (400m) and the **Junction Canal** (300m) to the next road (200m). ❊

⑪ Cross to the pavement and go over the bridge along the road to the ***Parrot*** (100m).

⑫ Go over the grass in front of the pub (cross ditch at junction) and diverge R from the main road up between the trees (300m). If the grass is long follow the road.

⑬ At the Horsham road (A281) cross to the main green and walk over the cricket pitch to the parking place (200m).

10 Shalford and Chantries

About 7 km or 4½ miles; a scenic walk; steep hills, several stiles, no bad mud; soft sand in summer; much to see; good for winter walking. OS maps: 1:25000 145 Guildford; 1:50000 186 Aldershot.

Linking walks   9★ ⑫✪ ⑲☆ ⑳✪ ㉑✧ ㉕★ ㉖✿

Start from Chantries car park, Shalford, TQ 003 483 or from St Martha's Hill (Halfpenny Lane) car park, TQ 021 484. Shalford Station is near the route.

The Sea Horse ☎ 01483 514351   ***The Queen Victoria*** ☎ 01483 561733

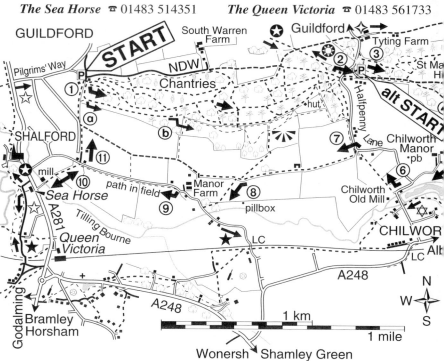

Walk into the **Chantries** gateway.

ⓐ *Alternative route, less shady: Keep on ahead on the main path over the end of the ridge then round L up the flank (800m).*

ⓑ *When the main path bends L again, find a narrow path R down into the field (100m) then ascend L through the Five Fields along the brow of the hill. At the end, beyond the hut, go L through the trees to a main path (1100m)* ✪ *then R up to the lane (50m).* ➔②

① Shady route: Turn L opposite the hut and climb onto the ridge. Keep on the same line along the undulating ridgetop paths always aiming for the highest ground ahead until you reach Halfpenny Lane (2000m). ✪

② Walk up the lane L (50m) then R up the footpath past houses to St Martha's car park (50m). ✧

③ From the carpark take the wide sandy track R up **St Martha's Hill** to the church (700m). ✿

④ Pass through **St Martha's Church**yard. Go out by the south gate (R from church) and straight down the very steep path to the end just after a house R (600m).

⑤ Turn R along the track to the tarmac drive and walk down past **Chilworth** Manor to Halfpenny Lane and straight on to the corner at Blacksmith Lane (600m).

⑥ Ascend on the footpath above Chilworth Old Mill (400m).

⑦ Turn L at the lane. Immediately enter the field L. Follow the cart track undulating along the L edge (400m), past the farm buildings R and over the rise (400m).

⑧ In the dip, just past the hill path back R (40m), cross the boundary L and take the diverging path over the field, through the hedge and down the steep slope to the lane near the **Tilling Bourne** (300m). ★ Walk up the lane R (250m).

⑨ Just after the drive to Manor Farm R enter the field L and follow the footpath from field to field beside the hedge next to the lane to the end near houses (600m).

⑩ Go down the field L and along the path to **Shalford Mill** (250m). If visiting the *Sea Horse* keep on along the drive (50m) ☆❶ then return to the top of the field.

⑪ Exit from the field, cross the lane and follow the track, opposite, which becomes a footpath between the fields R and road L (300m). When the road bends L carry on ahead over the foot of the hill to the car park at the **North Downs Way** (350m).

The entry for Shalford in the Surrey folios of the Domesday Book written 1086, actual size. TRE means before the Conquest, *Tempore Regis Edwardi*, in the time of King Edward (the Confessor). The line through SCALDEFOR was red for highlighting. A virgate was ¼ hide.

Robert holds SCALDEFOR from Richard. Two brothers held it TRE. Each had his own house but they remained one court; They could go where they would. Then & now it rated for 4 hides. Land for 6 ploughs. In lordship are 2 ploughs; 29 villagers & 11 smallholders with 9 ploughs. A church; 10 slaves. 3 mills @ 16s; meadow 4 acres of pasture. Wood @ 20 pigs. Of these hides one man-at-arms holds one virgate, where he has half a plough & 1 slave & 5 smallholders. Total value TRE £16; later £9. Now £20. To this manor belongs 1 property in Guildford @ 3s.

11 Chinthurst Hill and Blackheath

About 8 km/5 miles over Greensand hills with good views; soft sand when dry; half shady. Allow time for confusion on the Blackheath paths.
OS maps: 1:25000 145 Guildford; 1:50000 186 Aldershot.

Start from Chinthurst Hill car park, TQ 014 462, or Blackheath village car park, TQ 036 462.

Linking walks   9◇   12★   34✦   ㉕❖   ㉗✪   ㉜✳   Dorking
                                                      Silent Po
                                                      Albu

The Grantley Arms ☎ 01483 893351
The Villagers ☎ 01483 893152

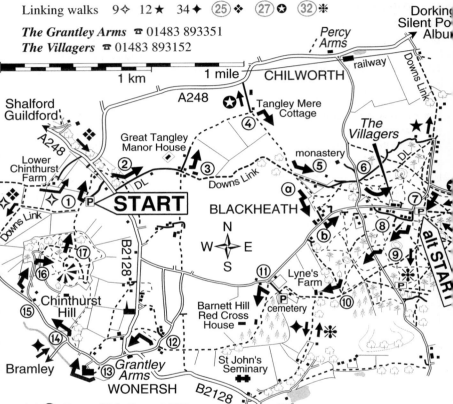

✧❖① From **Chinthurst Hill**
follow the Downslink route: cross to the footpath outside the car park and follow it down to the main road (200m).

② Cross into the path opposite. Follow it R (200m) and join the lane L past **Great Tangley Manor House** (400m).

③ After the drive L (100m), at the 4-way junction of tracks and path, go L past the buildings and on

around the bottom of the hill to Tangley Mere Cottage (700m). ✪

④ Go past the house, around the R bend and up between the fields to a 4-way path junction (500m).

ⓐ *Alternative though **Blackheath** village: Walk straight on between the gardens (200m) then fork R and keep to the boundary down past houses to the road (200m).*

22

(b) *Walk up the road past church (100m), and crossroads (100m) to the **Villagers** pub (200m) and on into the car park (200m).* ✦⑧

⑤ Turn L and stay on the track to the lane (450m).

⑥ Cross the lane and take the narrow path R of the Downslink track opposite. Keep on until near the war memorial L (300m). ★ To visit the pub take the path down R (250m); otherwise stay on the same path to the lane (250m).

⑦ On the other side, slightly R (20m), take the path through the scrub to the car park (100m). ✳

⑧ From the road exit of the car park turn L along the track to the cricket field (100m) and cross to the pavilion (150m). Turn along that edge of the field away from the houses and go straight out on the heathland path until level with a slight hillock L (150m).

⑨ Take the side path R which branches at a right angle down to the road (100m). Cross to the path opposite and keep on up, over tracks on the ridge (200m) and down the other side to a junction of bridleways (200m).

⑩ Go L (20m) then on down the steep path from the junction (200m). ✦ At Lyne's Farm ignore the valley path L and carry on up the other side, climbing the L bank when possible to the footpath. Pass along the edge of the cemetery (300m) then take the track L & R to the road (200m).

⑪ Turn back L up the cart track past **Barnett Hill** house (400m) and down to **Wonersh**, emerging beside Woodyers (600m).

⑫ At the road cross to the green

R (30m) then follow the L edge to the main road (150m) and go L to the road junction at the Pepper Pot and **Grantley Arms** (200m). Turn R along The Street (200m).

⑬ Turn off L through the covered gateway (see the frieze) and pass over the memorial garden to the church then return to the road via the church drive (200m). Carry on along the road past the ancient house, Green Place, R, and out of the village (200m).

⑭ At the bend take the lane R up the hillside, **Cranleigh Water** visible below L (350m).

⑮ Between houses on top, bear R up Chinthurst Hill drive (300m).

⑯ Cut across the hairpin bend and take the steepest path up to the tower on top (200m).

With your back to the tower door the great distant eminence almost ahead (SE) is the Leith Hill range. The houses below, slightly L, are part of Wonersh and above them is Barnett Hill with the eponymous Red Cross house in the trees. Beyond it L, the Blackheath pines are visible further round the ridge. If the air is clear the South Downs may be visible far R.

As you descend, St Martha's Hill is ahead with the North Downs behind it and vehicles climbing to Newlands Corner R. Guildford Cathedral can be seen beyond the Hog's Back because of the notch in the chalk ridge where the River Wey passes through. The high ground on the skyline above the cathedral is Bagshot Heath.

---

⑰ The doorway faces SE. Walk northwards over the hill and find paths down towards the L edge of distant **St Martha's Hill** (300m). From the boundary, walk straight down to the car park (200m).

12 Blackheath and Albury

About 8½ km/5¼ miles on the Lower Greensand over hilly heath, woodland and pasture. The Blackheath paths are confusing. Shady in summer; a good winter walk. OS maps: 1:25000 145 Guildford; 1:50000 186 +187.

Start from Blackheath village car park, TQ 036 462. Chilworth railway station is near the route.

Linking walks   11★ ㉖❁ ㉗✛ ㉘✳ ㉚✿ ㉜✳

The Drummond Arms ☎ 01483 202039   **The Villagers** ☎ 01483 893152
The Percy Arms ☎ 01483 561765.

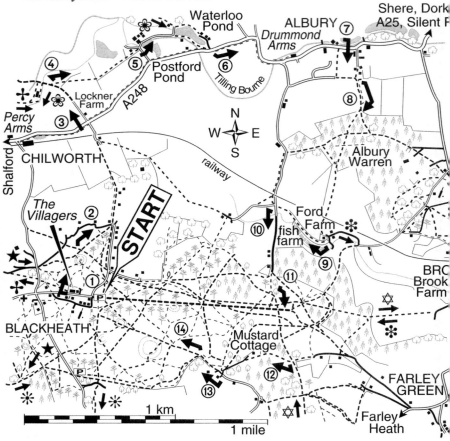

✛★① From **Blackheath** car park go down the lane and R into the **Villagers** car park (200m). Don't continue on the path parallel with the road but take the one from the top R corner. Keep on uphill to the

war memorial on its hillock (300m). ② Go straight down the other side (50m) then bear R on the bridleway, across a junction (40m) and ahead to a corner of the heath near houses (300m). Cross the track into the path beside the garden and keep on down the hillside then on tarmac over the railway to the main road (800m). The **Percy Arms** and Chilworth Station are 500m L along the road.

③ Cross and walk down the track past Lockner Farm (400m). 🐝

④ Just before the bridge turn off back R through the fields (site of the Admiralty gunpowder works), past a pond L and a garden to **Postford** Pond (650m).

⑤ Follow the lane over the bridge L, past houses (which replaced Postford Mill) and on (250m). At the bend take the path R between the ponds (or the next path R) to the road (250m).

⑥ Follow the main road L all the way to the **Drummond Arms** in **Albury** (700m). Carry on though the village past the mill (300m) and the trout pond (150m).

⑦ Where the road bends L, turn R into the estate office drive (if the office is open ask to see inside the pigeon house) then walk on to the top and up the path (200m).

⑧ At the path junction in the wood either go on up the sunken track or, better, climb to the corner of the field above L and follow the edge above the sunken track, rejoining it at the gate near the top (200m). Just before the wood fork R out of the sunken track over the hill top (200m). Cross a track and carry on down to the edge of the plantation (300m). In the field go L along the fence past the corner of the wood and straight down to the railway (300m). Cross and descend into the sunken path which curves L past the garden of **Ford Farm** house (150m). ✳

⑨ At the drive turn R (10m) and R again into the field. Keep to the R side of the valley to the next lane (450m).

⑩ Turn L. Pass over the brook, up the sandy lane to the last house (500m) ✿ and go straight up the middle path (200m).

⑪ Over the brow bear L on the crossing track which curves R and crosses several forest tracks. Keep on ahead over a slight rise then down to the 4-way path junction in the hollow (near a garden fence L) (600m).

⑫ Turn back R up the slope past Mustard Cottage R (250m) and carry on ahead on the sandy drive (other tracks join from R) round down L to other houses (250m).

⑬ Turn R. Follow the boundary track from the end of the tarmac until it bends L (200m). ✳

⑭ Take the straight track ahead over a rise (300m) and on (200m). Just before the next rise and the crossing track, fork R to the car park (200m).

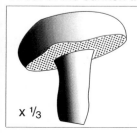

x ⅓

Boletus has many species which grow on heaths and are easily recognised: mainly brown with stout stalks, deep caps and pores in place of gills. Most are edible but best left for famine years; one is poisonous. Their hyphae (threads) attach them to birch or conifer roots, for mutual benefit, in the symbiotic partnership called *mycorrhiza*. Fungi are like plants and animals in their DNA but best considered a kingdom themselves, with the moulds and yeasts. Bacteria have different DNA.

13 Cutt Mill, Rodsall and Elstead

About 8 km or 5 miles mainly over farmland; fairly shady but with soft sand and nettles in summer; avoid in very wet seasons.   OS maps: 1:25000 145 Guildford; 1:50000 186 Aldershot.

Linking walks   1✦   6❀   14✪   22◉   23✿   27❀

Start at Elstead, SU 905 435 (layby near the church), or Puttenham Common Top car park, SU 920 461.

The Golden Fleece 01252 702349
The Woolpack 01252 703106
Elstead Mill   01252 703333

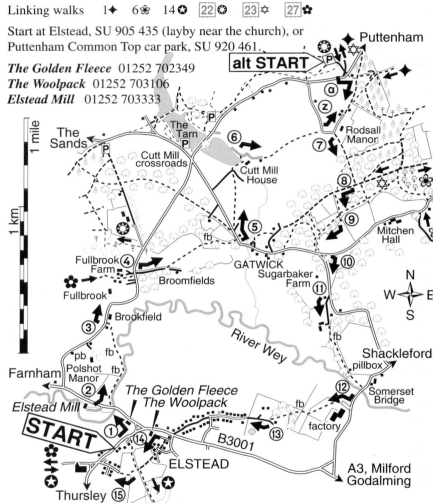

① From the parking layby in **Elstead** walk along the road to the Green (300m)(the ***Woolpack*** is R). Bear L past the shops and L along the main road. Cross Elstead Bridge to the riverside path R (350m). Go into the drive to see **Elstead Mill** then return.

② Follow the footpath along the River Wey then straight on to the next road (650m).

③ Turn R up the road which curves R then L (500m). ✪

④ Opposite Fullbrook Farm turn R and follow the Broomfields track to the gate L (200m). Enter the field L and cross diagonally R, along the depression. Keep on into the wood to **Gatwick** (500m).

⑤ At the road go L (100m) then ½R on the path diverging from the farm track after the house. Cross a track and walk along the dam of Cutt Mill Pond, round the corner to the boat house and R onto the drive at **Cut Mill House** (600m).

⑥ Turn R and follow the drive to Willow Cottage. Carry straight on along the bridleway to the end at the lane (500m) and go R (100m).

② For Puttenham Common go on to the end of the tarmac (100m) then up the sunken track (300m) and take the footpath up L. ✿✦

ⓐ If starting from **Puttenham Common** Top car park, cross the road to the house and skirt R of the garden to the sunken track (100m). Descend the bridleway R (300m) then the tarmac (100m).

⑦ At the bend below **Rodsall Manor** take the path L (400m). ✾

⑧ At the T-junction go R (150m) then L on the 1st side path (120m).

⑨ Just before the field turn R on the path in the trees (150m). Keep on along the edge of the wood or field to the road junction (200m).

⑩ Walk down Attelford Lane past Sugarbaker Farm (400m).

⑪ At the 1st house (Horseshoe Cottage) bear R on the farm track. After the buildings keep on slightly L into the wood, across the foot bridge, past a **pillbox** and over the field to **Somerset Bridge** (550m).

⑫ Walk over the bridge along the road (100m), R through factory car parks and diagonally L across the field to the furthest corner then R along the path (600m).

⑬ Join the track and continue between the houses on Ham Lane into Elstead (650m).

⑭ Go over the main road into the road opposite, R along Back Lane past the 1st house then L up the hill to the gate on top (400m). ◐

⑮ Ignore the path L. Go down the path R outside the field and on to the crossroads at **Elstead Church** (200m) ✿ then R to the layby.

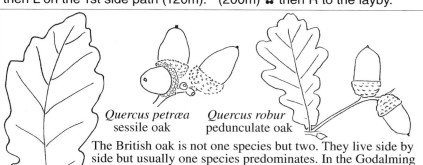

Quercus petræa
sessile oak

Quercus robur
pedunculate oak

The British oak is not one species but two. They live side by side but usually one species predominates. In the Godalming area most are *Quercus robur*, the pedunculate oak, so called because its acorns are on stalks - *peduncle* is the botanical term for a fruit stalk. *Quercus petræa* is sometimes the more abundant in western parts and has sessile (stalkless) acorns in a cluster at the tip of the twig. The leaf stalks are the other way round: *Q. robur* leaves are usually almost stalkless while *Q. petræa* has stalks of 1 cm or more. The leaf blades are very variable in shape and size - less helpful for identification. x½

14 The Moat, Lion's Mouth and Elstead

About 9 km/5½ miles; best in early morning when the heather is flowering (August); mainly heathland and fields with little shade; several short hills and stiles; soft sand in summer. Allow time for confusion on the heath.
OS maps: 1:25000 145 Guildford; 1:50000 186 Aldershot.

Linking walks 13✪ 15✷ 27✡ 28✦ 30❄

Start from The Moat car park, SU 899 416, or in Elstead, SU 905 435 at the layby on the Thursley road between the Green and the church.

The Golden Fleece ☎ 01252 702349
The Woolpack ☎ 01252 703106

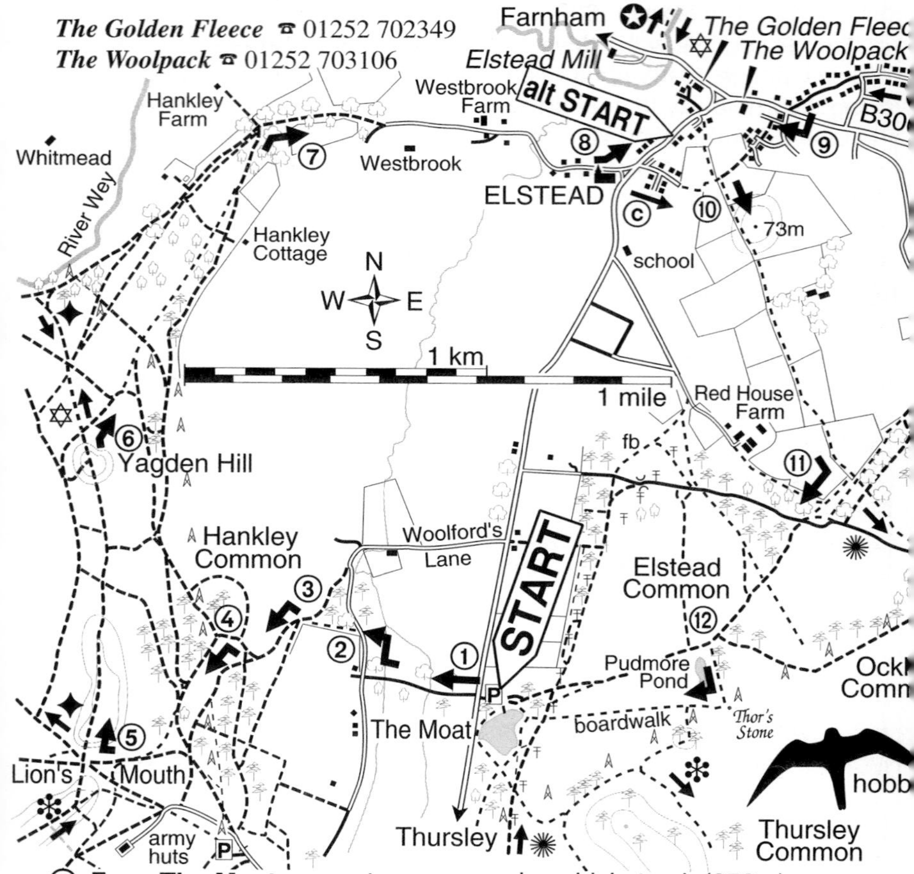

① From **The Moat** car park cross the road and follow the track, opposite, to the end (400m).

② Go R along the lane to the end of the fence L (150m). Turn L along the fence under the trees (200m).

③ Emerging on the heathland of Hankley Common, go L along the main vehicle track (250m).

④ Turn off R up the next broad track to the T-junction (200m) then L (150m) and diverge R on the track curving up though the trees (400m). ✦ (If confused or for a short cut, go straight up through the heather to the ridge top.)

⑤ At the Lion's Mouth (a notch in the ridge) climb the path R and walk northwards along the ridge (towards Crooksbury Hill telecommunications tower on skyline) and over **Yagden Hill** (1100m). ✡

⑥ From the brow descend the N path (80m) but turn R down the track at the foot. When it curves R (200m) carry on ahead, under the power cables (200m). Disregard tracks L & R and continue to a 5-way junction under trees (800m).

⑦ Disregard Hankley Farm track ahead. Go R along the main track then on along the lane past Westbrook Farm to the road junction at **Elstead Church** (1400m).

ⓒ *Cut of ¾ km/½ mile missing Elstead and pubs: Cross and walk up West Hill then the path beside the field to the track junction on top. Turn R (300m).* ➧⑩

⑧ Turn L to the Green ✪ and the ***Woolpack*** (400m). Carry on along the main road (200m).

⑨ Turn R at the next side road, Springfield, and R again into Back Lane then take the path L after the 1st house, up the hill (400m). At the junction on top turn L.

⑩ Follow the footpath along the R edges of the fields. One field before the wood ignore the gate in the corner but go on 50m from the corner (1200m). ✺

⑪ Just before the gate to the wood, cross the fence R and go down through the wood to the broad gravelled track (250m). Cross and continue ahead on the horse track across the heath to Pudmore Pond L (500m). You should be walking almost parallel with cables on pylons 400m L.

⑫ Just before Pudmore Pond are two footpaths L. Take the 2nd, on the boundary mound of **Thursley Common** (200m). ❄ Follow the R bend and go straight over Thursley Bog on the mound with sections of boardwalk (600m). Cross the wide path with electricity poles and carry on ahead to the edge of the Moat pond (100m) then R round the edge to the car park (150m).

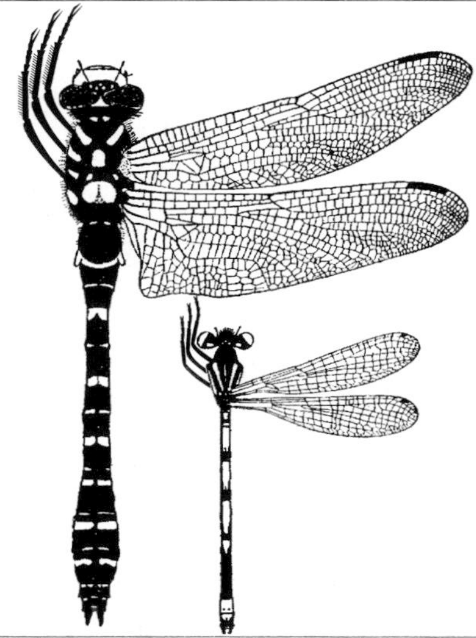

Thursley Common has the richest dragonfly and damsel-fly fauna in Britain. These two groups make up the insect order Odonata. They are the hawks of the insect world and catch other insects on the wing with forward mounted legs. The juveniles are wingless and aquatic, and prey on water insects and crustaceans.

Slender form distinguishes damselflies, but they may be longer than small dragonflies. The classification is based on wing form. Dragonflies have different fore and hind wings which are spread at rest. Damselflies have similar wings fore and aft, held up and pressed together at rest.

The Dragonflies of Great Britain & Ireland C O Hammond Harley rev 1996 116pp

15 Thursley Common and Village

About 8 km/5 miles; best early in the morning when the heather is flowering; good birdwatching; heathland, woodland and ponds; undulating; soft sand. The heath paths provide only poor landmarks so allow time for confusion. OS maps: 1:25000 145 Guildford +133 Haslemere; 1:50000 186 Aldershot.

Linking walks   14✳   16✦   17⊙   18✿   19✳   30★   32❀

Start from The Moat car park, SU 899 416, beside the Elstead/Thursley road or at Thursley recreation ground, SU 899 398 (park on the grass near the children's play area), or at the Old Portsmouth Road car park, SU 497 394.

No pub.

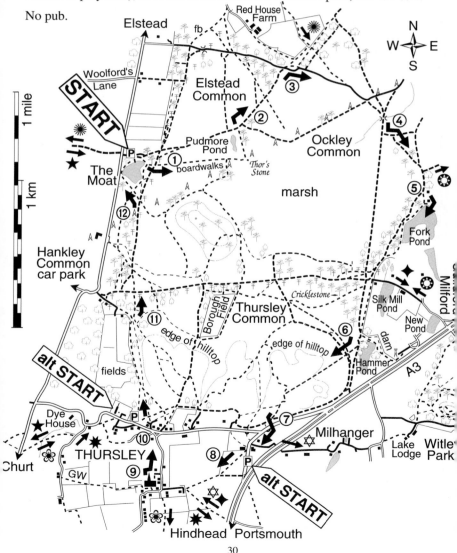

30

✳①　At **The Moat** follow the pond edge away from the road (150m). After the 1st marshy corner take the footpath L and cross the sandy track with the electricity posts (50m). Continue ahead on the **Thursley Common** Nature Trail which becomes boardwalks. After Pudmore Pond L keep on to the bend at Thor's Stone (600m) then L to the parallel bridleway (200m).

②　Follow the bridleway R to the hard, gravelled track (500m).

③　Go R along the track, around L & R bends and on to the L bend just after the pylons (600m). Don't follow this bend but continue ahead (200m) over the stream.

④　After the stream (100m), take the branch track L (50m) then turn off R. Ignore a path converging L and the nearby fenced track L ❂ (250m) and keep on (150m).

⑤　When the path bends slightly R, fork L onto the lesser path and follow the edge of Fork Pond until a boundary brings you back to the the main path (500m) then follow the fence L. When the main track diverges R keep to the smaller path beside the fence past the house ✦ (250m) and re-join the main track where the fence bends L (400m). Continue ahead past two small paths L until the **Hammer Pond** is visible L (100m).

⑥　Fork R up the side path which crosses two curving paths (100m) and ascends the hill. This was the London to Portsmouth Road! On the brow (250m) look back then continue over the flat top to the edge of Thursley Common (450m).

⑦　Turn R on the boundary track but find a gap L and join the road as soon as possible (50m). Go on along the road and turn down Old Portsmouth Road to the houses L (former *Red Lion*)(200m). ✿

⑧　On the other side of the road, near the shed, take the footpath across the field to the diagonally opposite corner (250m) and carry on up the next field in the same line to the house (250m). ✳ Walk down the drive to the lane (150m) and ahead up to **Thursley Church** (100m). ★❀

⑨　Walk round the church and leave by the north gate (100m). Turn L along the lane to **Street House** and fork L (300m).

⑩　Cross the road into the track between houses. When it bends R (30m) keep straight on down the path (200m). Join the converging path and go down L to the field (100m). Carry on beside it (500m).

⑪　When the path bends L at the end of the field don't stay on it but take the path ahead down to the wide sandy track (200m). Cross and carry on (500m).

⑫　After the pylons bear L on the crossing path and follow it round The Moat to the car park (300m).

 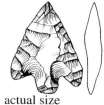

actual size

Flint arrow heads found on the slopes of Thursley Common by local people. They may be Neolithic but flint tools persisted into the Bronze Age. Dating to 2000BC is very approximate.

Drawn by Audrey Graham

© Surrey Archæological Collections <u>86</u> 1999

16 Thursley, Hammer Pond and Cosford

About 7½ km/4¾ miles; best at dawn when the heather is in flower; heath, farmland and ponds; undulating; soft sand in summer; nasty road crossings. OS maps: 1:25000 145+133; 1:50000 186 Aldershot.

Linking walks 15✦ 17❖ 18✿ 19☆ 20☆ 30❂ 32★

Start at Thursley recreation ground, SU 899 398. Park on the grass near the children's play area. No pub.

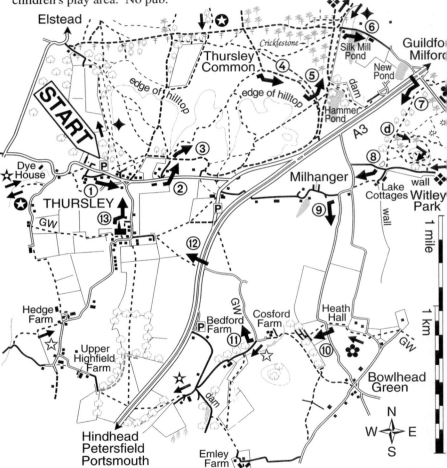

❂✦① From Thursley recreation ground walk up through the village past **Street House** at the junction (100m) and on (200m).

② Just before the 1st field R turn L down the track at Foldsdown Cottage (200m).

③ Cross the boundary track of **Thursley Common** and fork R. The path winds across the flat top (500m) then drops and joins a wide track near a bend (300m).

④ Follow the wide track R, round the bend and on (400m).

⑤ Ignore minor side paths but go L on the next wide crossing track down to the **Hammer Pond** (100m) and on along (L) the wide track beside it (100m). When it bends a bit L take the lesser path ahead, along the fence (350m). ❖

⑥ At the cottage turn on the track past Silk Mill Pond. At the drive (350m) keep on ahead round New Pond to the main road (250m).

⑦ Cross the dual carriageway ❀ into Lea Coach Road (50m) and turn off on the path R. It curves away from the main road past a path back L (400m) (see ⓓ) and ends at a track junction (300m).

ⓓ *Detour through part of Witley Common owned by the Herpetological Conservation Trust: Follow the path up the L flank of the hill. Skirt R round the crown of the hill back to the original path.*

⑧ Cross the broad track and continue up the drive past Lake Cottages (100m) then up the sunken path to the end (150m).

⑨ Go L on the lane (100m), round the bend and ahead to the S-bend before Heath Hall house (1000m).

⑩ The route now follows the **Greensand Way** to Thursley: At the end of the S-bend take the crossing footpath R over the field (150m) and down the escarpment, The path bends R on each terrace before dropping again (100m). At the bottom of the slope carry on along the path and round L up past **Cosford** Farm (200m). ★☆

⑪ Follow the tarmac drive up to the main road (700m).

⑫ Go over the dual carriageway and on along the path between the fields (200m) then on over the field towards the house (200m). Follow the drive down to the lane (150m) and keep on ahead up to **Thursley Church** (100m).

⑬ See the church then find the path out of the churchyard on the north side (100m) and follow the lane L back to the recreation ground (400m).

Commons are usually open to the public for air and exercise but are not owned by the public or by the nation. They are remnants of land called *waste* in early documents which was not ploughed for crops but used for grazing, firewood, peat cutting, building materials, etc. As the population became denser the waste was divided between communities who marked boundaries with mounds or hedges in medieval times. The land now belonged to the lord of the manor and commoners; they could use it for themselves but not work it for private profit or sell it.

For enterprise there was a tendency in the Middle Ages for shared arable land to be parcelled by agreement into private farms and much of the waste was taken up at that time. If a few commoners resisted the majority, they were overcome later on by individual Acts of Parliament. Only village greens and the least useful commons survived. Surrey has large commons because of its extensive heaths.

In the 20th century commons lost sight of their commoners; a commoner might have the right to graze two cows but was not allowed to fence them and would not want to herd them; coal replaced peat and firewood; &c. By default, lords of the manor became the only visible owners and were able to dispose of commons. In Surrey they sold to boroughs, builders, the Army, preservation societies and the Forestry Commission. There are still a few commoners with registered rights.

The Common Lands of England & Wales W G Hoskins & L Dudley Stamp 1963 Collins

17 Witley Common, Bagmoor and Moushill

About 8 km/5 miles but variable; two half-mile extensions; mainly heathland and woods; undulating. Be warned: the heath paths are very confusing.
OS maps: 1:25000 145 Guildford +133 Haslemere; 1:50000 186 Aldershot.

Start from the National Trust car park, SU 932 406, signposted off the A286.
Several other car parks are near the route.

Linking walks 15❂ 16❖ 18✳ 21✴   *The White Lion* ☎ 01483 421116

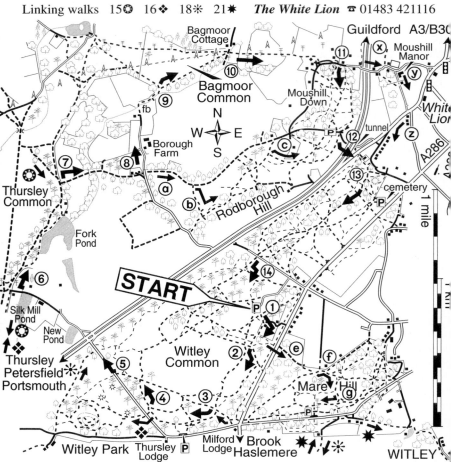

① From the car park walk to the corner of the NT building (100m) then R up to the corner of the boundary mound (100m).

ⓔ *Extra ¾ km/½ mile over* **Mare Hill***: Turn L beside the mound to the road (150m). Cross and go up the track. When it enters a garden*

keep on outside (300m).

ⓕ *Swing L on the path round the houses (100m) then fork R (100m) and take uphill paths R (150m).* ✳✴

ⓖ *Follow the ridge path R to the crossroads (600m). Go on over the main road (70m), R down the path from the road (100m) then L.* ➧③

② After the mound (30m) fork L to the T-junction (80m). Go L on this path (100m), round a R bend to a crossing path (400m). Go L up to another cross path (80m) and on.

③ Continue round the top of Witley Common (paths L are from the little car park)(400m). ❖

④ Eventually curve down R and join a converging path (100m) to the 4-way junction (200m) then go L to the road (200m).

⑤ Follow the road R (300m). Cross the dual carriageway and continue along the side road. Just after New Pond when the tarmac becomes a private drive (200m), fork L on the track past Silk Mill Pond to the end (350m). ❍

⑥ Turn R on the wide heath track. When the fence curves R (250m) take the small path down R which skirts Fork Pond then rejoins the main track (500m). Go on (200m).

⑦ Take the track R between hedges and over a rise (600m). After the house fork L (30m).

ⓐ *Wet season alternative: Cross the tarmac drive and take the track ahead curving R & L (400m).*

ⓑ *From the L curve take the well-worn R uphill path to a junction on top in the trees (200m). Follow the main path L out of the wood and down the flank of the hill. Ignore a track forking R (200m) and carry on into a pine grove past two crossing paths (300m).*

ⓒ *After the 2nd (200m), turn R up the wide path curving L past a white house (300m). Don't fork R but stay ahead all the way to the car park or, after electricity poles, take branch paths R over the heath to the car park (300m).* ➔⑫

⑧ Turn L on the drive (public footpath) to Borough Farm. When the tarmac ends go on past another house (400m), over a footbridge then R beside the brook (250m).

⑨ Fork R. Stay on this path along the edge of Bagmoor Common and past the house L (550m).

⑩ Continue ahead through the field then between fields, curving R near houses (650m). Turn L on the track outside the field (100m).

ⓧ *Extra ¾ km/½ mile: Go L past the house, ahead on the lane over the A3 and round bends (400m).*

ⓨ *Turn R through the gate of Moushill Manor and stay ahead up to the main road (300m).*

*The **White Lion** is L (150m).*

ⓩ *Go up the road R (200m) and diverge L on Sandy Lane (200m). Round the L bend, just after the pump house fence, turn R on the side path (50m) then L.* ➔⑬

⑪ Go L past the house (40m) and R, opposite the end of the garden, up the steep path (100m). On the brow take the path up L to the top of Moushill Down (120m), round R and down to the car park (250m).

⑫ Exit from the car park down under the A3 (50m). After the tunnel turn R on the side path and cross the road (50m). Follow the path R of the pump house into the trees (100m) and ahead.

⑬ Ascend (80m). Don't fork L over the top (to car park) but stay on the main path over the edge of the hillock. Keep to the path ahead to the disused road (900m).

⑭ Carry on opposite (120m) and take the 1st side path L (120m). On the L curve take the side path to the NT car park (200m).

18 Thursley and Brook

About 9½ km/6 miles; short cuts can be made if starting from Brook; heath, pasture and woodland; one short steep ascent; two crossings of the A3.
OS maps: 1:25000 145 Guildford +133 Haslemere; 1:50000 186 Aldershot.

Linking walks   15✿   16♣   17✳   19✳   20✳   21★   30 ❖   32 ✤

Start from Thursley in the Old Portsmouth Road car park, SU 497 394, or from Brook in the service road beside the A286, SU 929 383, or from the Witley Common car park beside Lea Coach Road, SU 926 398.

The Dog & Pheasant   ☎ 01428 682763

♣ On the Old Portsmouth Road walk away from the A3.
① Turn R on the track after the houses (former *Red Lion*). Go down to the road (200m), over the dual carriageway and ahead. Disregard all side tracks. Go down between the gardens, past **Cosford Mill**, round the bends and up to the lane (700m).
② Go L on the lane (100m). At Heath Hall drive when the lane curves L, take the path ahead, down to Lake Lodge (200m). Continue down the drive (100m).
③ Cross the wide track and keep on ahead into Witley Common. ✳ Take the side path R (200m) or a lesser path before it. Head for the small hill then follow the track round the R flank (500m). Beyond the hill, join the oblique crossing path from L to the road R (150m).
④ Cross and go into the next part of the Common (50m) then take the path R up round the top, over the 1st crossing path (300m) (from the car park R) to the 2nd (200m). Turn R up to the crossroads at Milford Lodge (150m). Cross the main road. Take the path under the trees parallel with and L of the side road (200m). Fork L and keep on to the top of **Mare Hill** (300m).★

⑤ At the cross path with electric cables go R to the car park (80m). Walk over the road and on down through the trees, slightly L, to join the track at the houses (100m). Go past the houses and straight up the fields; the footpath curves up the small valley between the hills (900m). Cross the last field ½R to the farm buildings (100m).
⑥ Skirt L round the barns (100m) and take the track L to the bend at Parsonage Farm Cottages (200m).
⑦ Turn R along the path (500m). Bannicle Hill semaphore was up L.

⑧ After the field turn L, not up beside the field but diagonally onto the flank of the hill and follow the path to the road (400m).

ⓘ *If visiting the **Dog & Pheasant** take the branch path over the hill and cross the cricket field (300m).*

ⓙ *Return along the L edge of the cricket field and through the end of the wood (300m).*

⑬ Cross the lane. Go straight over the field (150m) and down the escarpment; the path bends R on each terrace before dropping again (100m). At the bottom of the hill go on along the path, round L and up past the house (200m).✳️❀

⑭ Follow the tarmac drive up to the main road (700m).

⑮ Cross the dual carriageway

(map)

Guildford, Witley Common — Milford — Mare Hill
③ ④ Thursley Lodge — Milford Lodge
lhanger — wall — P
② Lake Lodge — Witley Park — alt START — A286 — ⑤ ★
osford Mill
Ⓢ
N W E S

Heath Hall — Parsonage Farm — ⑥
⑬ ⑫ GW ⑪ — alt START — ⑨ — Bannicle Common — ⑦
Bowlhead Green — ⑩ — ⑧ — GW — ✿ site of semapho... tower
BROOK ⓙ — ⓘ
Dog & Pheasant
Haslemere

1 mile
1 km

⑨ Cross the main road and walk along Screw Corner Road (400m).

⑩ At the 1st house R go through the wall, up the hill and between the fields on top (300m).

⑪ At the end follow the track R (300m). When it bends down the valley go on up the hill (100m), through the wall, across the drive and over the small fields (200m).

⑫ Cross the lane into the field. Follow the R edge past gardens (150m) then cross the fence and follow it L (100m).

and go on between fields (200m) then diagonally R to the house (200m). Follow the drive down to the lane (150m) and keep on to **Thursley Church** (100m). ❖✿❀

⑯ Visit the church then find the path out on the N side (100m). Go R on the lane to the bend (100m).

⑰ Return up the drive L to the house (150m) then cross the field, ½L to the near corner of the small field beyond (250m). Continue on the diagonal right of way to the shed or exit via the track (200m).

19 Thursley to Highfield

Short route 5½ km/3¾ miles; longer version 9 km/5½ miles over farm land; hilly; many stiles; nasty road crossings. Many variations possible.
OS maps: 1:25000 133 Haslemere; 1:50000 186 Aldershot.

Linking walks   15 ✳   16☆   18✳   20❄   30 ◇   32 ✳   33 ♣

Start at Thursley recreation ground, SU 900 398; park on the grass near the children's play area. Near Hindhead a small car park, SU 895 367, is close to the route on the lane to the Punch Bowl youth hostel.   No pub.

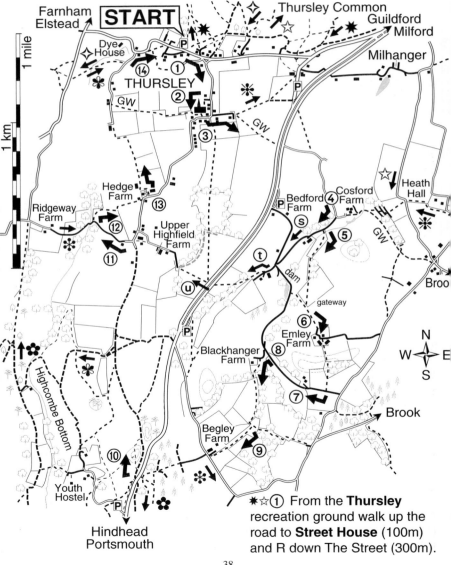

✳☆① From the **Thursley** recreation ground walk up the road to **Street House** (100m) and R down The Street (300m).

② At Wild Goose Cottage take the track R to **Thursley Church** and leave by the S gate (100m).

③ Go L down the lane to the bend (100m) and on ahead up the drive (150m). ✳ Two paths cross the field diagonally from the end. Take the R one (400m). Cross the dual carriageway and go on down the tarmac drive (300m), round the R bend and down to the L bend (400m) just before houses.

④ Turn R down the track to the side path L (100m).

⑤ *Shorter route: Stay on the track to the 4-way junction (400m) and into the farm ahead (100m).* ⓣ *At the house drive go R on the path up the flank of the hill. Don't go into the field but on up the flank (150m). In the hilltop field go ½L over the crest to the road (150m).*

ⓤ *Cross the dual carriageway into the field opposite and go straight over aiming for the gap in the trees. Join the track (300m) and follow it up R past the barn. At the next bend take the footpath L diverging over the farmyard to the lane (400m). Cross and go down the side lane opposite.* ➔⑪

⑤ Longer route: Turn L over the stream and go up round the top of the field, out at the top R corner (250m), along the edge of the wood (150m) and up to the top corner of the next field (200m). Join the path outside the field and go L continuing on the track which bends into Emley Farm (250m).

⑥ At the farmhouse turn R between the barns and go up the field beside the R hedge (200m). Keep on in the same line over the hill down to the track (200m).

⑦ Follow the track R to Blackhanger Farm L (500m).

⑧ Turn L down the drive (100m). Just before the garden enter the field L and skirt the garden to the top corner (100m). Cross the belt of trees to the next field (40m) and follow the L edge (300m).

⑨ At the end, exit L to the path junction (30m) then go R along the boundary (200m). Cross the last field to the R corner and go out to the lane (100m). ✳ Slightly R (20m) walk up the forestry track. Disregard side tracks and keep on up the steepening path to the main road (500m). ❧

⑩ Cross the road to the track slightly L and follow it up R. A small path L leads over a hillock with good views then back to the track. Carry on along the track on the ridge, down over the crossing track (900m) ✳ and on to the lane junction (750m). Turn L.

⑪ Follow the lane and track down to the stream (300m).

⑫ Don't cross but enter the field R and follow the L edge above the stream then up the hill to the top L corner (250m). Go out along the path between fields (200m).

⑬ On the lane go L but almost immediately (30m) turn off L along the footpath beside the drive of Hedge Farm. Go round the garden (100m) then R, down between the fields, with L & R bends, to the lane (600m) ✧. Keep on ahead down to the road (600m).

⑭ Follow the road R until it bends L uphill (100m) then go straight up the path ahead and over to the recreation ground (200m).

20 The Devil's Punch Bowl and Highfield Farm

About 8 km/5 miles; heath, pasture, woodland; long ascents; many stiles.
OS maps: 1:25000 133 Haslemere; 1:50000 186 Aldershot.

Linking walks   16 ☆ 18 ❋ 19 ❋   30 ◇   32 ★   33 ◆

Start at Hindhead, SU 890 357, from the large (pay) car park almost opposite
the Devil's Punch Bowl Hotel.

Devil's Punch Bowl Hotel
☎ 01428 606565

Devil's Punch Bowl Cafe
☎ 01428 608771

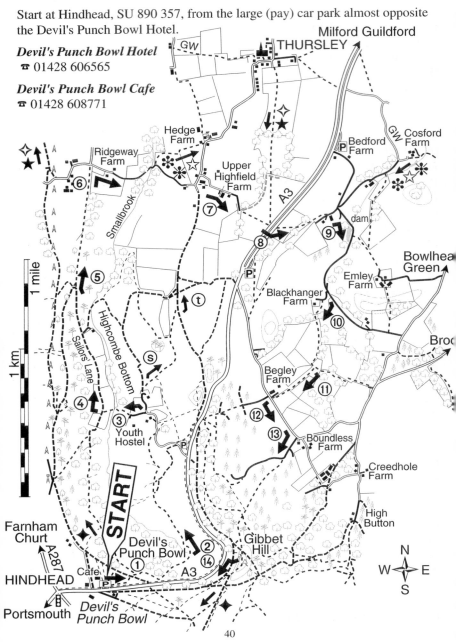

① From the **Hindhead** car park walk over the grass, parallel with the main road to the broad path on the rim of the **Devil's Punch Bowl** (100m). Cross it and go on. Ignore a path down L (30m) ✦ but at the bend near the road (150m) descend the stepped path L to the spring in the narrow valley (350m).

② Carry on ahead, undulating around the side of the combe, ignoring all side tracks (800m). At the end go L down the tarmac lane past houses (200m).

Ⓢ *Short cut: Turn down R past Gnome Cottage (200m). Just after the cattle grid take the path R up the valleyside eventually past a field on top (700m).*

Ⓣ *On the ridge track go L down to the lane (900m) then R.* ✦⑦

③ Don't follow the R bend of the tarmac but go straight down the track past the Youth Hostel, over Smallbrook (200m) and up to the T-junction (100m).

④ Turn R and follow the track past the fields (500m) then on up the side of the valley (400m). ★✧

⑤ On top of the ridge, when the main track bends L, continue ahead along the ridge; the horse track soon sinks into a deep stony cleft between fields, at first grey Hythe sandstone then brown Bargate sandstone (800m).

⑥ At the end go R on the tarmac lane up past the houses and on down the rocky track to the stream (450m). ❀❀☆ On the other side of the valley, stay on the track up past the house and ahead (300m).

⑦ At the top cross the lane and take the footpath through the Highfield farmyard to the farm track and carry on past another house and down (400m). At the bottom enter the field L and go straight up the slope and over to the main road. The line of the footpath is often unclear (300m).

⑧ Cross the dual carriageway into the field opposite and go ½L over the brow and down to the exit near the midde of the bottom edge (150m). Carry on down through the trees to the farm house (150m) and walk out of the drive L (100m).

⑨ At the track junction go R, past the pond (200m) and on to Blackhanger Farm (500m).

⑩ Turn R down the drive (100m). Just before the garden enter the field L and skirt the garden to the top corner (100m). Cross the belt of trees to the next field (40m) and follow the L edge (300m).

⑪ At the end, exit L to the path junction (30m) then go R along the boundary (200m). Cross the last field to the R corner (100m).

⑫ Join the lane and walk L to Boundless Farm (300m).

⑬ Just before the 1st house turn R up the track (200m). At the R curve keep on up the lesser track ahead, over a cross (400m) and round L. When the path flattens, ignore a side path R and cross a track (250m) then ascend to the flat top of **Gibbet Hill** (100m).

⑭ From the trig point take the level track (SW) to the main track on the edge of the hill (Old Portsmouth Road)(120m). Go L down it, past the **murdered sailor**'s stone R (100m), to the end at the main road opposite the car park in Hindhead (700m). The ***Devil's Punch Bowl Hotel*** is L (50m).

21 Witley, Enton and Sandhills

About 8km/5 miles; through farmland, heath and wood; undulating; half shady; suitable for winter walking. OS maps: 1:25000 133 Haslemere; 1:50000 186 Aldershot.

Start from Witley Lodge, SU 945 396, near Witley Church. Witley Station (in Wormley), SU 948 379, is on the route and has free parking at weekends. There is a car park and roadside parking near Sweetwater Pond, SU 953 390.

Linking walks   17✱   18★   22✿   23✳   26❀

The White Hart ☎ 01428 682554   **The Wood Pigeon** ☎ 01428 682362

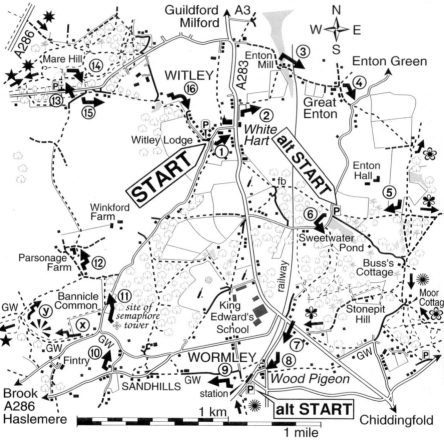

① From Witley Lodge walk down the lane past **Witley Church** to the **White Hart** (200m) then go L along the pavement of the main road to the end of the high wall opposite (200m).

② Follow the footpath between the wall and the house, Lashams (250m). Before the cottage enter the corner of the long field and diverge from the L boundary down to the L house (200m).

③ Exit to the track. Cross **Enton** mill-stream and follow the winding track past the houses, under the railway (100m) and up to the T-junction (300m).

④ Go R (150m), over the lane and ahead up the footpath into the field (150m). Cross the R corner into the next field (100m) then aim ½L, over the brow of the hill and down to the bottom corner near the house (300m). ❀ Cross the drive and go on along the bottom of the next field past the pond (300m). Enton Hall is up R. Keep on ahead (150m), out of the field and through the heath, forking R, to the track junction (100m). ❀❀

⑤ Turn R along the path through wooded heath. Carry on beside the field and out through the little car park to the lane (500m).

⑥ Go L along the lane across the end of Sweetwater Pond (100m) then turn off L along the winding footpath through the wood. Ignore all side paths (500m). At the end follow the garden boundary out to the track from the house (100m) and go L to the main road (150m). Notice **King Edward's School**, R.

⑦ Cross and carry on along Combe Lane (400m).

⑧ At the ***Wood Pigeon*** turn R to Witley Station (100m).

⑨ Cross the station footbridge. Keep on along the platform to the end (100m) and out R up the track to the 4-way junction (150m). Take the track L to the end (400m) and continue ahead on the path out past houses (250m) then along the lane to the crossroads in the hamlet of Sandhills (250m). The field L is good for picnics.

⑩ Walk R up Sebastopol Lane (200m) then L up the next lane to the T-junction on top (250m). ★

ⓧ *Extra 500m: Go L (70m) and take the path R above the lane. Follow it around Bannicle Common (taking the view through gaps in the hedge) to the bottom (400m).*

ⓨ *At the bottom join the path along outside R (500m).* ↴⑫

⑪ Go R along the lane to the 1st field L (100m) then diverge L on the path under the trees (200m). At the end turn L (150m).

⑫ Turn between Parsonage Farm Cottages to the farm (150m) then skirt R round the barns to the next track (100m). Cross the narrow field diagonally R into the little valley (100m) and follow it down, R of the dividing fence (600m). Cross a field track and go straight on to the house and past it (250m).

⑬ Don't follow the R bend in the drive but go straight up through the trees to the road (100m) and on through the parking layby to the crest of **Mare Hill** (100m). ❀

⑭ Follow the ridge path R (100m) and return to the road on the 1st side path R (100m).

⑮ Cross into the track opposite and go L past the houses (150m) and on down the footpath ahead (not the one diverging L)(300m).

⑯ At the bottom cross the drive of Lower Roke and continue ahead between gardens then R across the end of the pond (100m). Up the steps, take the path L through the wood round the flank of the hill and up (200m). On top carry on along the straight path, or the lane beside it, to Witley Lodge (300m).

22 Witley, Hambledon and Wormley

About 7½ km/4¾ miles; mainly heath and wood; undulating, half shady, good in winter. OS maps: 1:25000 133 Haslemere; 1:50000 186 Aldershot.

Start from Witley Lodge, SU 945 396, near Witley Church or from Hambledon Church, SU 970 389. There is a car park and roadside parking near Sweetwater Pond, SU 953 390.

Linking walks 21✾ 23✾ 26✦   *The Merry Harriers* ☎ 01428 682883
The White Hart ☎ 01428 682554

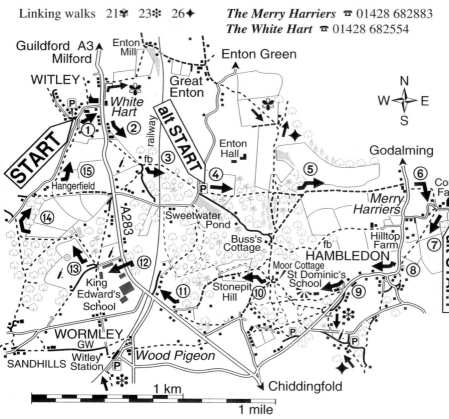

① From Witley Lodge walk down the lane past **Witley Church** to the ***White Hart*** (200m) ✾ then go R on the pavement down the main road (200m).

② Cross to the recreation ground beside Chichester Hall and converge on the L boundary to the furthest corner (300m).

③ Join the track in the wood outside the field but turn L almost immediately (30m). Go down the footpath beside the garden, over the footbridge, under the railway (100m) and on to the road (300m).

④ Carry straight on over the road, past Sweetwater Pond car park and along the edge of the wood eventually to a broad cross track (500m). ✦ Still continue ahead through the wood to the end of the broad bridleway (200m).

44

⑤ At the end join the crossing bridleway and go L, round the R bend (60m) and on between fields to the road at the ***Merry Harriers*** at **Hambledon** (700m).

⑥ Continue on the footpath opposite the pub up to the lane near Hambledon Church (300m).

⑦ Cross the lane and climb the bank into the field. Walk down through the middle and out of the furthest corner. Stay on the same line down to the house (500m).

⑧ Walk down the road past the junction (100m) in the middle of the village and on (300m). ❋

⑨ Diverge R up the path beside the boundary of St Dominic's School to Hambledon Common. Ignore all L turns and keep on along the path round the flank of the hill to Moor Cottage (500m).

⑩ Walk along the track from the house (50m). Turn R on the bridleway and immediately L steeply up to the top of Stonepit Hill (200m).

Go straight over the flat top, R of the house (100m), and out down the drive to **Wormley** (600m).

⑪ Cross to the pavement and follow the main road down R, over the railway (200m) and up past **King Edward's School** (300m).

⑫ After the school and houses turn L along the drive (200m).

⑬ At the end of the tarmac take the path R: not the one back beside the cricket field but the other. Follow this under trees to the pond (250m), round a L bend and on (100m). Watch out for a path forking R and follow it up beside the field (300m). Above the fields join the larger path up R to the lane (150m).

⑭ Follow the lane R (300m).

⑮ Just after the large house, Hangerfield, watch out for a side path R. Follow it beside the lane down to the next house and keep on down the drive to the parking area at Witley Lodge (500m).

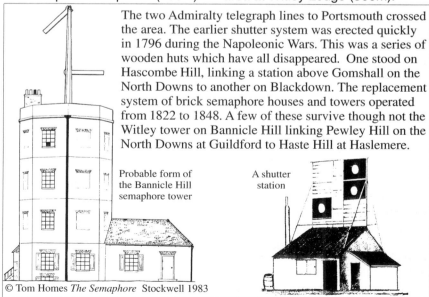

The two Admiralty telegraph lines to Portsmouth crossed the area. The earlier shutter system was erected quickly in 1796 during the Napoleonic Wars. This was a series of wooden huts which have all disappeared. One stood on Hascombe Hill, linking a station above Gomshall on the North Downs to another on Blackdown. The replacement system of brick semaphore houses and towers operated from 1822 to 1848. A few of these survive though not the Witley tower on Bannicle Hill linking Pewley Hill on the North Downs at Guildford to Haste Hill at Haslemere.

Probable form of the Bannicle Hill semaphore tower

A shutter station

© Tom Homes *The Semaphore* Stockwell 1983

23 Hambledon Hurst and Chiddingfold

About 8 km/5 miles extending by 1½ km/1 mile; mainly through woods, undulating. The Hurst tracks are too muddy for winter walking.
OS maps: 1:25000 133 Haslemere; 1:50000 186 Aldershot.

Start from Hambledon cricket green, SU 963 380, where there are only a few parking places. At weekends parking is free at Witley Station, SU 948 379.

Linking walks 21✳ 22✲ 24✪ 26❖ 33✪

The Wood Pigeon ☎ 01428 682362   ***The Winterton Arms*** ☎ 01428 683221
The Crown ☎ 01428 682255   ***The Swan*** ☎ 01428 682073

① At **Hambledon** follow the path out of the corner of the cricket green furthest from the road. Go along the garden fronts, past **Oakhurst** into the wood, **Hambledon Hurst**. Disregard a side path L (100m), and go on, over a little humped bridge (500m), to the path junction just before the fence of an industrial site R (200m).

② Turn L along the horse track. Watch out for boundary mound beside it R (350m) and continue to the path junction after it (150m).

③ Fork R. Disregard the many side turns. The path swings L to pass fields (350m) then R down to the valley bottom (400m). ◉◉

④ Turn R over the horse bridge. Keep on ahead along the valley, past the side bridge L (200m), to fields (450m) and the road at the **Winterton Arms** (300m).

ⓔ *Extension to* **Chiddingfold** *village green: Go L along the road (300m). At the R curve take the path L up between gardens. In the fields follow the L edges (300m).*

ⓕ *At the top path go through the hedge L then R beside it, over the field and out to the lane (400m).*

ⓖ *Walk down the lane (R) and along the green past the* **Crown** *to* Chiddingfold Church *(400m).*

ⓗ *Follow Coxcombe Lane, L of the pond, to the end (500m).*

ⓘ *Slightly L (50m) cross the road and take the track after the club (150m). Cross the field to the far end (200m). Enter the field L.* ➔⑥

⑤ Cross the road and take the path opposite the pub, over the stream (200m) and on under trees between fields (450m). At the little stream crossing enter the corner of the field R.

⑥ Diverge from the L fence to the middle of the far side (100m). Keep on through the trees (150m).

⑦ Go R up the road (50m) then R up the path, past gardens (150m). Carry on along the L edges of the fields (350m), down through the wood and over the streams to the fields (200m). Ascend round the flank of the L hillock to exit near the top L corner of the field (150m).

⑧ Walk towards Noddings Farm (50m) then cross the field diagonally to the bend in the middle of the R side (100m). Go over the footbridge and over the next field to the far L corner (200m) then follow the path L through Minepit Copse and over a strip of field to the road (300m).

⑨ Enter the field opposite and cross diagonally R to the corner with the trees (100m). Go on under the trees then between warehouses and a housing estate (200m). Keep on at the edge of the next wood. Ignore side turns L and ultimately pass through the garden of Lilac Cottage to the railway (250m). ✳✳

⑩ Follow the road R past the station and ahead round to the **Wood Pigeon** (200m). Cross Combe Lane and take the path opposite the pub, between gardens to the road (500m).

⑪ Cross slightly L (30m) and walk up Wormley Lane (300m). At the bend take the track ahead (100m) and turn R at the 1st side path.

⑫ Fork L up the steep bank and follow the path through the heath above the sunken track, rejoining it before the house (250m). ❖

⑬ Walk down to the R corner of Moor Cottage, R past the garage and up the main path (200m). On top don't fork L but descend round the flank to **Hambledon** (300m).

⑭ Cross the road to the track along the house frontages below and go R down the curving footpath to the village shop (150m) and cricket green.

24 Chiddingfold and Stonehurst

7 km/4½ miles extending by 1½ km/1mile; wood and farmland; undulating; half shady. The path through the wood is too muddy for winter walking. OS maps: 1:25000 133 Haslemere; 1:50000 186 Aldershot.

Start at Chiddingfold, parking at the bottom of the green, SU 961 354.

Linking walks 23✪ 33✪

The Winterton Arms ☎ 01428 683221
The Crown ☎ 01428 682255
The Swan ☎ 01428 682073

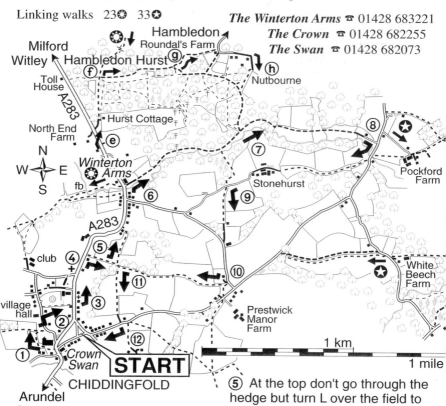

① At the corner of **Chiddingfold** green near the *Crown*, cross the main road into the churchyard. Follow the hard path. Beyond the church turn R to the field (200m).

② Go R along the track (70m), L along the road (200m) and R through the recreation ground, back to the main road (200m).

③ Follow the road L, past the cricket field (200m) and on (150m).

④ Turn R up the cart track beside the house, The Croft (250m).

⑤ At the top don't go through the hedge but turn L over the field to the hedge bend. Keep on down the R edge, out between gardens (300m) then R along the road to the *Winterton Arms* (300m). ✪

ⓔ *Woodland extension of 1½ km/ 1 mile: Carry on beside the main road (450m) and turn off R on the drive to Hurst Cottage (100m). Cross the grass in front of the house and continue on the path through the wood to the 4-way junction near the fence of an industrial site (250m).*

48

(f) *Turn L along the horse track. Watch out for boundary mound beside it R (350m) and continue to the path junction after it (150m).*

(g) *Fork L and keep on round L and R curves then beside Roundal's Farm (350m).*

(h) *At the tarmac lane go R and ahead on the track (250m), round the R bend up to the field (100m). Take the path skirting R of the field (200m). Join the woodland path down L to the valley bottom (300m). Turn L. →(7)*

(6) Go down the track twixt bridge and pub, through the yard and on along the footpath between fields (250m) into the wood. Ignore the side path R (500m) and a side path L just after a bridge (200m).

(7) Carry on through the wood (250m) then along the narrow fields. Follow the trend of the L boundaries (350m). In the last field aim for the house beyond it (200m) and go out along the track past the house (100m). ○

(8) Turn back along the lane R (150m). Just over the bridge before the next house turn off R along the path between fields (600m). At the top join the track skirting R of the Stonehurst Farm buildings (200m). At the tarmac drive keep on round the double bend and up to the crossing path after the paddocks (200m).

(9) Go through the field L up the L boundary (250m) and out down the track (200m). Carry on along the lane L up to the next house R, Rystead (250m).

(10) Cross the driveway into the trees a few steps (50m) then turn R along the track to the fields. Go up the L boundaries (300m) then into the field L and on in the same direction at the R edge (400m).

(11) At the end don't go on through the hedge but L round the corner and straight over the field, out down the track to the lane (400m).

(12) Walk down the lane (250m) and along Chiddingfold green.

The **glass-making industry** of England started around Chiddingfold. Glass-blowers appear among Egyptian hieroglyphics but any British skills departed with the Romans. There is no evidence of any permanent industry before the 13th century though the Saxons had imported vessels and Bede writes of glass workers being brought from Gaul in the 7th. The first evidence is a deed of 1226 granting land to Laurence, *Vitrearium* de Dunkeshurstlonde (Duns Farm) and the same man re-appears in 1240 supplying glass for the new Westminster Abbey. The early makers were Flemish and French. Locally the industry faded after the use of timber was proscribed in 1620, but it spread elsewhere under the same families. The Loseley Papers include an inquiry of 1569 into a fracas between glass-makers in which a red hot glass-making rod found application.

Sand by itself will melt at 1710°C to form silica glass but this temperature was beyond the early makers. Soda or potash provided sodium or potassium which allowed sand to melt at lower temperatures, reacting to form silicate glass. The early glass houses used bracken ash for potash. A 2:1 mixture (by bulk) of ash and sand was heated in stout clay pots in a wood fuelled furnace. Window panes were cut from discs, up to 60 cm in diameter, made by fast spinning of blown bulbs. The sand came from local outcrops in the Weald Clay and from the Greensand; the landscape was dominated by coppiced timber for fuel.

Wealden Glass 1226-1615 S E Winbolt Combridges 1933 85pp

25 Tuesley to Hydon Heath

About 8 km/5 miles on the Lower Greensand; fields, heath and coppice; half shady, stiff climbs. OS maps: 1:25000 145 + 133; 1:50000 186 Aldershot.

Linking walks   26☆   30✳

Start at Hydon Heath car park, SU 978 402, or near Milford Hospital, SU 962 418, or in Ashstead Lane outside Ladywell Convent, SU 968 425.

No pub.

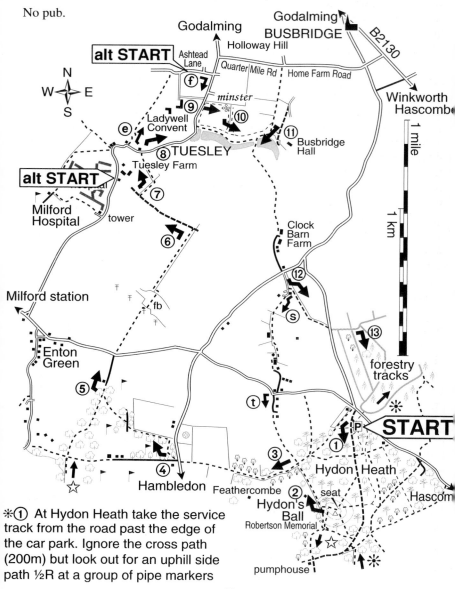

✳① At Hydon Heath take the service track from the road past the edge of the car park. Ignore the cross path (200m) but look out for an uphill side path ½R at a group of pipe markers

50

(150m) and climb it to the summit of **Hydon's Ball** (300m). ☆

② Turn R across the flat top away from the trig point and the Octavia Ball granite seat and drop to the path passing on that side of the hill (100m). Go R, along the boundary down to the cross path at the fence corner (350m). Turn L.

③ Follow the path down the flank of the hill through coppice then between fields to the road (900m).

④ Don't go along the track on the other side but the path ½R from it. Cross a tongue of the golf course (150m) then turn L along the fence in the trees and keep on after the field (200m). At the track take a few paces R (30m) then go on as before over more golf course to the path in the trees (300m).

⑤ Turn R to the track and carry on to the road (300m). Cross to the footpath opposite and keep on beside the garden. Go straight over the field to the wood (400m), R (50m) then through the wood L (100m). Then return to the original line and cross the next field beside the boundary, R (500m).

⑥ Turn L along the cart track towards the farm (400m).

⑦ Before the barns turn R along the field boundary (150m) then L along a mound to the lane above **Tuesley** Manor House (200m). (**Milford Hospital** is up L 500m.)

ⓔ *Extra 600m: Go L up the lane (100m) and take the footpath R beside the 1st house. Cross a small valley then ascend between fields to the next lane (600m).*

ⓕ *Go R on Ashtead Lane to the end (300m) then R down Tuesley Lane to the 1st field L (200m).* ↪⑨

⑧ Turn R and follow the lane down into the valley (400m) and up the other side (200m).

⑨ Opposite the back gate of **Ladywell Covent**, enter the field and go along the top edge to the shrine which marks **Tuesley Minster** (100m). Carry on round the corner of the field and down to the next corner (200m).

⑩ Turn L through the wood. Keep to the level paths and avoid side paths up L or down R (300m).

⑪ At the end join the sunken path down between the ponds then up the other side of the valley to Clock Barn Farm. Continue along the drive to the road (800m) then along the drive opposite (150m).

ⓢ *Short cut if not making for Hydon Heath: Take the footpath L after the 1st house and follow it along the field boundaries, R & L round the shed then out on the house drive to the lane (800m).*

ⓣ *Take a few paces R on the lane (20m) then turn L up the drive past the houses (150m) and keep on up to the major crossing path at a fence corner (350m). Turn R.* ↪③

⑫ Before the 1st house turn off L along the bridleway and cross the road (400m). Go along the forestry track opposite (private but tracks used by walkers). Ignore the path 1st R but turn at the cart track 2nd R (150m).

⑬ Follow this round a R bend (400m) and on to a broad U-bend L (200m). Watch out for a narrow side path, R, halfway round the bend. Exit across the road into Hydon Heath car park (50m).

26 Hydon's Ball to Hambledon

About 7½ km/4¾ miles or 5¼ km/3½ miles over heath and fields on the Lower Greensand with good views. Good winter and summer; half shady, hilly. There are several places with confusing paths so allow time for getting lost. OS maps: 1:25000 133+145; 1:50000 186 Aldershot.

Linking walks 21❀ 22✦ 23❖ 25☆ 30✳ 31✿

Start at Hydon Heath car park, SU 978 402, or Hambledon, SU 970 389, parking at the church (not Sundays) or at the *Merry Harriers*.

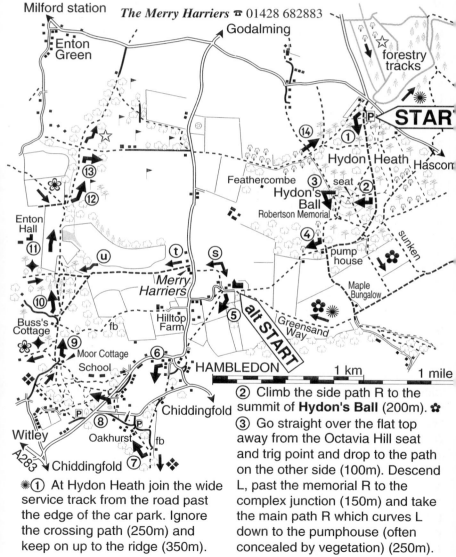

The Merry Harriers ☎ 01428 682883

✳① At Hydon Heath join the wide service track from the road past the edge of the car park. Ignore the crossing path (250m) and keep on up to the ridge (350m).

② Climb the side path R to the summit of **Hydon's Ball** (200m). ✿
③ Go straight over the flat top away from the Octavia Hill seat and trig point and drop to the path on the other side (100m). Descend L, past the memorial R to the complex junction (150m) and take the main path R which curves L down to the pumphouse (often concealed by vegetation) (250m).

52

④ At pumphouse junction take the path R (150m). Turn L to the fields and cross to **Hambledon** Church (600m). Go on along the lane past the church and Court Farm to the next house R (100m).

⑤ *Short cut or detour to the pub: Turn R on the drive past the house and carry on down round to the* **Merry Harriers** *(300m). Return or*

ⓣ *Take the track beside the pub between the fields (700m).*

ⓤ *After it bends into the wood (70m) turn R to the crossing track (200m) & R to the field (100m).* ➜ ⑪

⑤ Don't go on down the lane but up the bank L into the field. Walk down through the middle and out at the furthest corner. Keep on in the same line down to a house (500m). Go down the road (100m).

⑥ Turn L at the junction then fork R on the lane past the house fronts and go on down the path (250m). Over the road take the diverging path across the front of the house (300m). At the drive go L (100m). ❖

⑦ At the next house L turn back R, past **Oakhurst** to the green (200m) and cross it diagonally to the shop (200m). Go up the path between pond and shop to the track on top with houses (200m).

⑧ Climb the grass bank, L, to the road and take the path, opposite, up L onto the Common. Walk up between the trees around the L flank of the hill to Moor Cottage. Don't turn downhill at all and don't go straight up the hill (600m). ❀✦

⑨ From the cottage follow the drive out to the main track (50m) then take the bridleway R. Ignore the steep L branches and carry on down to Buss's Cottage (300m).

⑩ At the cottage don't follow the drive but fork R. Ignore the 1st L back to the drive (40m) but go L on the next fork to a crossing path with overhead cables (300m). Keep on ahead to the field (100m).

⑪ Continue straight over the field (100m) and on along the R edge past the lake, then out to the footbridge R below the house (300m).

⑫ Cross the brook and go up through the wood then follow the edge of the golf course L to the cart track (350m). ☆

⑬ Turn R along the track past the club buildings (300m) to the road (400m). Cross to the track on the other side and carry on between fields (400m) and up and through the woods below Feathercombe on the flank of the hill (400m).

⑭ At the crossing path beside the fence down from Hydon's Ball R, keep straight on, ignoring side paths, to the road next to Hydon Heath car park (500m).

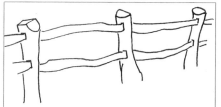

The rustic fences of NW Surrey are made from chestnut coppiced on a 30 year cycle. The posts are whole or ½ width logs, the rails ¼ or ⅛, split by hammer and chisel. Coppicing has survived because the steep Greensand slopes have little commercial use. In the past large areas produced charcoal for iron making. In 1667 John Evelyn estimated Sussex had 200 000 acres under coppice. Coke was not used for smelting until 1707.

27 Thorncombe and Nurscombe

About 7½ km/4¾ miles through tranquil country; hilly, in and out of the combes. The paths are well shaded; views better when the leaves are off the trees. OS maps: 1:25000 145 Guildford; 1:50000 186 Aldershot.

Linking walks 8☆ 28❖ 34✳ 35✿ 37◆

There is no ideal parking place. Start in Thorncombe Street layby SU 999 421 or park on the verge in Alldens Lane on the brow of the hill, SU 989 424.

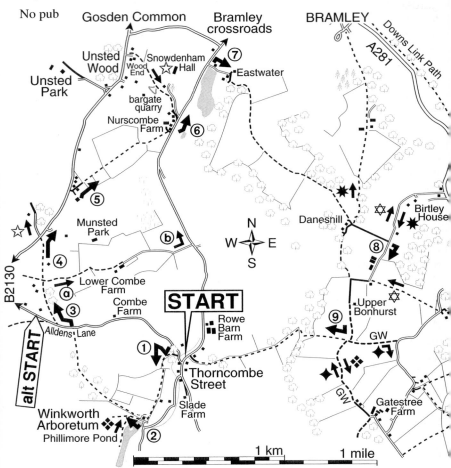

① From the Thorncombe Street layby walk down the lane (60m) and take the 1st R (70m). Over the bridge, turn L on the track through the trees (50m) and skirt L round the bottom of the fields (600m).

② At the end exit across the edge of the garden and walk along the drive past Phillimore Cottage and Phillimore Pond then on along field boundary (100m). Don't take any L turns (Winkworth

Arboretum) but enter the field R and go up the coomb beside the L boundary (200m). Carry on through the trees swinging R up the side of the combe then over the top to the lane (500m).

③ Walk L up the lane (120m) and take the bridleway R, below the garden, round the top of the field to the 4-way path junction (300m).

ⓐ *Alternative: Take the path R at field boundaries along the ridge to Lower Combe Farm (500m) and go on down the drive (500m).*

ⓑ *At the bottom follow the lane L to Nurscombe Farm (800m).* →⑥

④ Keep on down the path ahead (300m) ☆ then R down the lane past the drive of Munstead Park to the next houses R (400m).

⑤ Turn R into the shared drive. Go round the bend and on past all the houses then between fields, eventually descending into the combe. Join the lane outside Nurscombe Farm (800m). Turn L.

⑥ Stay on the lane, past the houses, down to the end of the large pond R (500m). The large house up L is **Snowdenham Hall**.

⑦ Turn R along the Eastwater drive. When it bends to the house (150m) take the track R round the barns (70m) and L up out of the combe then between fields up to the house Daneshill (1300m). ✳ Carry on straight down the drive to the T-junction (300m). ✿

⑧ Turn R up the farm track and follow it past the barns to the house (300m), round the R bend to the top (100m) and L to Upper Bonhurst (200m). Keep on ahead along the bridleway to the T-junction (250m). ❖✦

⑨ The bridleway R bends almost immediately. At the bend enter the field R and go straight up the spur of the ridge into the wood (200m). Follow the footpath up round bends R & L to the top (150m) then beside R boundaries up to and over the flat top field (350m) and down the other side. Descend at the edge of the grass rather than in the sunken path but watch out for the path to cross the fence near the bottom (200m). Carry on down and pass out beside the house to the lane in Thorncombe Street (150m).

A combe or coomb is a valley set in a hillside. The word, a rare remnant of the Celts occurs in place names like *Comp*ton and Welsh towns with *Cwm*. Coombs in this area descend abruptly on the escarpment at the edges of the plateau caused by the hard Bargate Sandstone overlying softer sands.

The Lower Greensand follows the lie of the chalk all around the Weald but only in this area does it have Bargate beds. The best large blocks, *doggers*, were quarried in the valleysides above Godalming and split into pieces like bricks. Further from Godalming the beds are of smaller, softer freestones used uncut and more susceptible to weathering. Galetting is a peculiarity of the Godalming area; small chips of ironstone help the mortar shed water.

Generally the use of stone died out about the time that lorries came on the scene so, if ordinary garden walls are made of stone, it must have been close by and easy to collect. Local hillsides have been scarped by stone collectors.

28 Winkworth and Thorncombe Street

About 8 km/5 miles extending by 1½ km/1 mile; tranquil but hilly farm land.
The route passes through Winkworth Arboretum but don't deviate from the
right-of-way unless you have paid or are a National Trust member.
OS maps: 1:25000 145 Guildford; 1:50000 186 Aldershot.

Linking walks 27❖ 29✿ 30✪ 32✳ 34✴ 35★ 37✪

The best starting point is Winkworth Arboretum car park, SU 989 412.
Thorncombe Street has a layby, SU 999 421. On the extension,
park opposite the *White Horse* in Hascombe, TQ 001 394.

The White Horse ☎ 01483 208258
Winkworth Arboretum NT ☎ 01483 208477

① Enter **Winkworth Arboretum** by the main path (400m). At the 3-way split take the stepped middle path and stay on the right-of-way down the R side of the little combe to the bottom (300m).

② Turn L. Keep to the path near Phillimore Pond ❖ then out round the end to the cottage (500m).

③ Don't join the lane but take the path L from the end of the tarmac past the garden and on along the bottom edge of the fields (550m). Around the curve in the 3rd field, exit by the gate R to the lane in **Thorncombe Street** (50m).

④ Go R to the junction (70m) then L (70m). Turn up the track beside the house R and continue at the edge of the field to the top (400m) then on along the L boundaries into the wood (500m). Descend R then L (150m). At the field go straight down on the spur of the hill to the track below (200m). ✻★

⑤ Now on the **Greensand Way**, follow the track R below the hill to Gatestreet Farm (700m). ❸

⑥ At the tarmac turn into the field R and follow the track round the L edge of the field and on (500m).

⑦ At the house drive R diverge R over the grass skirting the fence of **Wintershall** (200m). Cross the uphill track and carry on (100m) to join another track over the little valley. Go on across the field near the R boundary (300m) then into the wood and round below the hill fields to the lane (600m). ✿

⑧ Go R on the lane to the bend (70m) then turn up the track L to the 1st side track R (200m). ❸

ⓔ *An extra 1½ km/1 mile to* **Hascombe** *and the* **White Horse**:

Keep on ahead, over the cross track (GW) on top (200m) and, ignoring all side paths, along the hilltop and down (700m).

ⓕ *Pass between houses to the lane and carry on ahead, around the pond and past the church to the White Horse (450m).* ✲

ⓖ *Cross the field opposite the pub (150m). The Greensand Way goes on* ❸. *You turn R between the fields (200m).*

ⓗ *At the end go R to the drive from Hoe Farm (20m), R again (10m) then climb the bank. Pass the shed R and little pond L and follow the garden fence round the top (150m). Don't carry on into the next field but double back on the path R up into the wood (80m) then turn L along the path to its end at a track (300m) or cut the corner R.*

ⓘ *Turn R to the lane (100m). Cross and carry on ahead up to* **Hascombe Court** *(300m) and on along the lane (450m).* ↘⑪

⑨ Climb the steep side track (150m). Ignore the side track L on top and go down the other side. Pass two houses (350m) and keep on winding gently downwards (450m).

⑩ At the 3-way junction take the bridleway R towards the house (150m). Cross the main road and go up the steep track to the top (400m) then follow the lane L to the T-junction (200m). Turn R.

⑪ Keep on along the lane to the road (300m).

⑫ Walk along the main road R (150m). At the brow of the hill turn off L on the footpath to Winkworth Arboretum (600m).

29 Hascombe Hill and Scotsland Farm

About 7 km/4½ miles through woods and fields on the Lower Greensand with good views; shady; hilly. In winter the horse tracks become very muddy.
OS maps: 1:25000 133+134+145; 1:50000 186 Aldershot.

Linking walks 28✿ 30❊ 32✿ 37❖ 38❊

Start at Hascombe, TQ 001 394. Park on the verge opposite the *White Horse.*
(or on the verge 100m N of the fountain, SU 999 401).

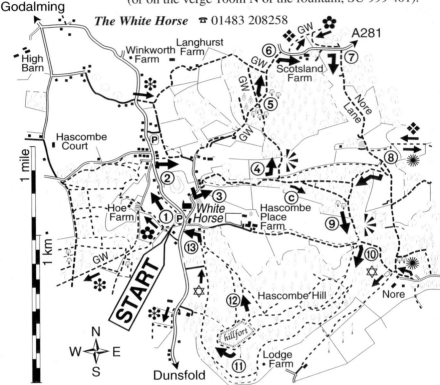

✿❊① Opposite the **White Horse** join the path outside the field and walk down R through **Hascombe** to the fountain L (500m).

② Opposite the fountain go along the footpath between the gardens, over the millstream and up the wider track to the lane (250m). Go R along the tarmac lane until it bends R (200m).

③ Turn L into the steep drive and take the bridleway beside it up the hillside. A footpath R cuts two corners and re-joins later. Carry on to the top of the fields L (600m).

ⓒ *Cut of 2 km/1¼ mile: Keep on through the wood (150m) then fork R to the junction on the edge of the hill (300m). Turn R.* ➜⑨

④ Take the side path L along the ridge between the fields (150m). Go on through the wood past the corner of a field (200m) down to the crossing track (200m).

⑤ Turn R and stay on this track down to the lane (400m). ❖

⑥ Follow the lane R, down past Scotsland Farm, up over the hill (200m) and down to the bottom of the 1st field (200m).

⑦ Turn R up the track below the fields (Nore Lane). Pass over a rise (500m), down to the pond R in the dip ✳ (200m) and on up to the sunken part under the end of the next field R (200m).

⑧ Climb the stepped path R to the top of the bank (10m) but don't go R up the edge of the field. Instead follow the path L along the top of the bank (50m) then turn R up the horse track. After a steep winding portion it bends L to the top (250m). Ignore the side track R here and the next (150m).

⑨ Carry on along the ridge track down to a 4-way junction (300m). ✿

⑩ Take the diagonal uphill path, which joins another (50m), up **Hascombe Hill**. Ignore the diverging path R (150m) and go on along the level path at the S (L) edge of the ridge. Pass a downhill path back L (300m) and the corner of the hill fort R (400m) and keep on to the end of the ridge (200m).

⑪ Follow the path as it bends R round the end of the hill (100m) then curves back along the other side (250m). Another R bend brings you to a path junction at the next corner of the hillfort (20m).

⑫ Turn L along the hill but immediately diverge on the downhill branch path. At the 3-way junction near the bottom (550m) bear R along the sunken path to the end near a house L (100m).

⑬ Go L down the tarmac drive to the *White Horse* (100m).

Hascombe Hill and Gibbet Hill are largely composed of the Hythe Sands. These form the stratum of the Lower Greensand below the Bargate beds and outcrop further to the south as they curve up into the Weald dome broken open by erosion. The dome was a ripple in the earth's crust when a collision of tectonic plates thrust up the Alps. The erosion that removed the chalk over the middle was most vigorous during the Ice Age.

The Hythe Sands lack calcium and do not retain water so they are covered by heath on hilltops where drainage is greatest. On the northern flanks of the hills the fields are on the kinder Bargate beds and the transition from grey (Hythe) to brown (Bargate) sand or stone is visible in worn paths.

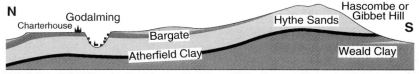

The Atherfield Clay is the lowest division of the Lower Greensand. It is rarely seen; it cannot stand out in valley sides as hard stone might. It causes the springs around the hills as water from the sand leaks over its edges. It forms dense clay soil which will not sustain typical crops because oxygen cannot move to the roots and microbes. Where the sand from the hills mixes with the clay the soil may be fertile, hence the fields south of the hills.

Greensand is misleading. It was a working title of early geologists for a series of predominantly sand layers, but limestones and clays interrupt the series.

30 Hydon's Ball to Hascombe

About 8½ km/5¼ miles or ½ mile more over heath and fields; hilly with good views. Good in winter but muddy; soft sand and overgrown paths in summer. OS maps: 1:25000 133+134+145; 1:50000 186 Aldershot.

Linking walks 25✳ 26✳ 28✪ 29✳ 31✳ 32✿

Start at Hydon Heath car park, SU 979 402, or at Hascombe, SU 001 394 - park on the verge opposite the *White Horse*.

The White Horse ☎ 01483 208258

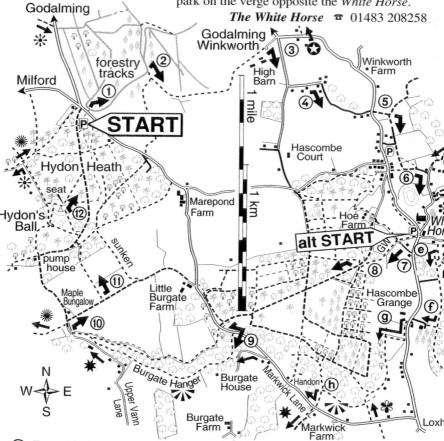

① From Hydon Heath car park take the footpath across the road into the forest (80m) and go R on the forestry track (550m).

② When the track curves L into a valley, take the path R. Ignore the side path R (80m) and carry on up beside the wood then along the house drive to the road (1100m).✪

③ Don't join the road but double back R on the narrow lane (350m) and take the 1st L (250m).

④ From the end garden take the track R down to the road (400m).

⑤ Go up the path opposite to the 3-way junction (100m) then take the track R past the house and drive R (200m) and on (100m).

Cut the corner over the fields via the path up L or keep on round the bend (100m) and up L (200m). ❊

⑥ After the house turn R along the tarmac lane, winding round the village pond and **Hascombe** Church to the road junction at the **White Horse** (500m). ❊

ⓔ *Extra 700m: Go up the drive beside the pub (100m) and R into the footpath beside the shed after the house. Climb the R bank and follow the parallel track (600m).*

ⓕ *Ignore the 1st R to the road but take the 2nd, from a rise (200m).*

ⓖ *Cross the lane L and go up into the field. Continue above the lane (100m) then cross to the top of the fields (150m). Follow the path L, outside the fields and under trees (500m). Go round the downhill bend (50m) and take the path R, along the hillside (300m).*

ⓗ *Descend the next L (150m).* ✳ *Walk R up the lane (400m) and L along the drive at Burgate Lodge (150m). After the bend (50m) go R over the grass up to the parallel path in the trees (50m) then L.* ➔⑨

⑦ Cross the road into the field opposite the pub. Keep on ahead, over a crossing path and along a

L boundary to the top L corner (250m) then into the wood and up the flank of the hill (150m).

⑧ At the brow of the hill take a few paces R (20m) to join another uphill path then follow that across the flat hilltop (**Greensand Way**) and down to the road (1000m). Do not continue opposite. Go L down the lane (100m) to another path R.

⑨ Follow this path along the bottom of the hanger past Burgate House and on (1200m). When near the lane join it or fork R up to the edge of the field but keep on ahead to the track junction near Maple Bungalow (200m). ✳

⑩ Turn R along the broad sandy track (300m).

⑪ Take the 1st L between fields which curves R at the end to meet a crossing track (400m). Don't join it but cross up to the next track (10m) then R, L, R up to the hilltop of **Hydon's Ball** (300m). ❊

⑫ Go down the path behind the Octavia Hill memorial seat back to the cart track (300m) and follow it down L to the car park (350m).

Gaultheria shallon on Hydon's Ball is a giant cousin of bilberry. Introduced from NW America for pheasant cover, it has no English name. Leaves 7-9 cm, finely toothed. Sprays of whitish buds in April. Flowers: June, 1cm white globes, Berries: September, 1cm black globes.

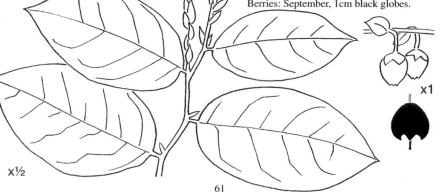

x1

x½

31 Dunsfold to Burgate Farm

About 7½ km/4¾ miles extending to 10½ km/6½ miles; farmland and woods at the edge of the Lower Greensand; good for spring flowers; half shady.
OS maps: 1:25000 133 Haslemere + 134 Crawley; 1:50000 186 Aldershot.

Start at Dunsfold, TQ 006 363, from the car park on the green.

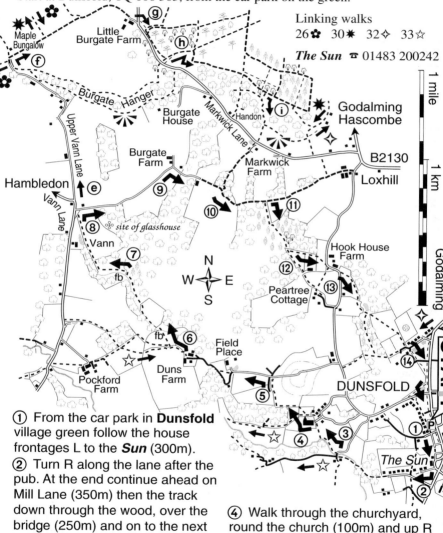

Linking walks
26✿ 30✳ 32✧ 33☆

The Sun ☎ 01483 200242

① From the car park in **Dunsfold** village green follow the house frontages L to the *Sun* (300m).
② Turn R along the lane after the pub. At the end continue ahead on Mill Lane (350m) then the track down through the wood, over the bridge (250m) and on to the next house (150m). ☆☆
③ Cross the bridge R (20m) and take the footpath L beside the stream to the well then R up to **Dunsfold Church** (250m).

④ Walk through the churchyard, round the church (100m) and up R to the adjacent small field. Cross it to the top L corner (100m). Pass into the next field and follow the L edge to the corner (150m) then up R to the tarmac drive (200m).

⑤ Turn L along the drive to Field Place (300m) then descend to the valley bottom either straight down the field or down the track L and round the hairpin (300m). Follow the track up the other side to the barns of Duns Farm (150m).

⑥ Next to the top barn, turn R on the path into the field (50m). Keep on along the edge to the gateway R (100m) and pass through to the field below. Don't turn L along the hedge but cross the field, in line with the gap, down to the bottom L corner (150m). Go out over the footbridge and L along the bottom of the fields (300m) then through the wood. Carry on near the stream to the footbridge (250m).

⑦ Cross and go up the valley side to the field (250m). Keep on along the L boundary past the house, Vann, to the road (350m).

ⓔ *Extension: Carry on ahead up Upper Vann Lane curving round houses (700m) to the sandy track on top (500m). ✿ The route now follows the* **Greensand Way**.

ⓕ *Turn R along the cart track in front of Maple Bungalow. ✱ Keep on over the rise and round down through Little Burgate Farm to the road (1100m).*

ⓖ *Cross to the path under the trees and follow it R beside the road up to the path crossing from the other side on the crest (300m).*

ⓗ *Go L up the GW to the oblique (1st) major cross track (250m). Turn off back R along that and round the bend (50m). Keep on past the side track L (350m) and watch out for a downhill path R (200m) in the chestnut coppice just before the next major track L.*

ⓘ *Turn R on this path to the T-junction (50m) then L down the steep winding path to the field (200m) ✧ and straight down the edge (100m). Cross Markwick Lane to the path opposite and go past the wall of Markwick Farm then on down the field track to the end (400m). Turn L.* ➔⑩

⑧ Turn R along the tarmac drive to Burgate Farm (700m).

⑨ At the junction near the house take the tarmac drive R to the barn R (200m) and carry on along the rough track to the double bend at the side track L (200m). ✧

⑩ Stay on the track round the bends to the footpath R at the end of the next block of woodland on the R (350m).

⑪ Turn down this side path under the trees. At the end of the field L (150m) take the L onward path through the wood into the corner of another field (200m).

⑫ Go L along the edge of the fields (200m), ½R over the last one (100m) and out along the lane R to the next bend (80m).

⑬ Enter the field L. Cross to the wood (100m) and go R along the curving edge of the field to the furthest corner (200m). Enter the adjacent field L and cut across the end into the dip (70m). Take the path down under the trees past the pond and up to the next field (50m). Cross to the furthest corner (250m). Go on along the L hedge past the next field (100m) and out L to the the green at Dunsfold.

⑭ Keep to the path at the R edge of the green round to the lane (450m). Cross and go along the frontages to the car park (200m).

32 Hascombe to Dunsfold

About 9½ km/6 miles; some steep paths, numerous stiles, excellent views over the Weald, soft sand in summer but half shady, bad mud in wet winters.
OS maps: 1:25000 133 + 134 + 145; 1:50000 186 Aldershot.

Linking walks 28✳ 29✿ 30❈ 31◇ 33★ 38❀

Start at Hascombe, TQ 001 394 (park on the verge opposite the *White Horse*), or at Dunsfold, TQ 006 363 (park in the village car park on the green).

The White Horse ☎ 01483 208258   *The Sun* ☎ 01483 200242

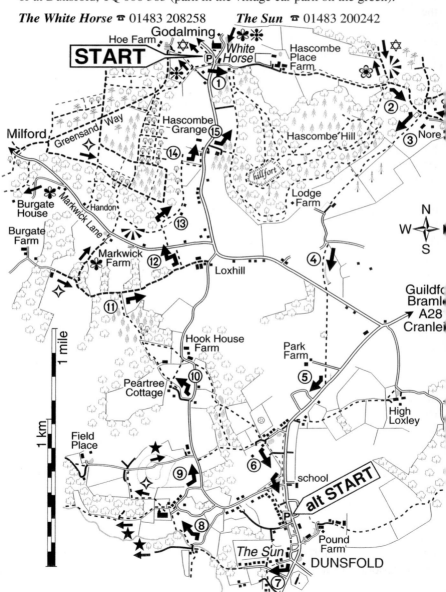

❄✿① Go up the drive R of the **White Horse** past the house and side path R (100m) and ahead on the track, past **Hascombe** Place Farm, and up. A path in the L field is nicer than the track (1100m). ❀

② On the ridge, admire the view.

> The great valley below is aligned with the notch where the Wey cuts through the North Downs at Guildford and was probably carved by the original river. Now, only a small tributary, Cranleigh Water, flows in it. The Horsham road follows this valley as did the railway and the Junction Canal. Winterfold is the hill opposite. Aircraft rising from Gatwick may be seen 15 miles away.

Carry on down steeply to the L bend at the next house. (If the bridleway is impassable after much rain, climb the L bank and follow that down) (300m).

③ Turn off up R past the tennis court and follow the path over the fields (the ring of standing stones L is modern) (1000m). By the barn walk out to the tarmac and carry on down the farm drive (200m).

④ Cross the road into the field opposite and go down R of the bushes and pond to the (nasty) road crossing (300m). Continue down the fields, past the lone tree, over the drive and, on the same oblique line, to the trees (600m).

⑤ Walk along the road R to the bend (350m) then cut the corner R to the lane past the ponds (200m).

⑥ Follow the R edge of **Dunsfold** green round and cross the next lane (450m). Keep on along the house fronts to the *Sun* (500m).

⑦ Turn R along the lane after the pub. At the end continue ahead on Mill Lane (350m) and down the track through the wood, over the bridge (250m) and on to the house L (150m). ★★

⑧ Cross the bridge R (20m) and take the footpath L beside the stream to the well then R up to **Dunsfold Church** (250m).✧ Walk round the church and back out.

⑨ Depart along the upper lane (300m). At the T-junction turn L and follow the lane past the farm house (250m) and on (350m).

⑩ Go up the drive L to Peartree Cottage and skirt the lawn to enter the field R of the house (100m). Follow the L boundary over a double fence and on along the 2nd field (400m). Carry on through the wood then out to a gravel cart track (400m). ❀

(❀ On Markwick Lane turn off along the drive at Burgate Lodge. Round the bend, the path goes up through the trees R.)

⑪ Go R along the track almost to the farm buildings (450m).

⑫ Take the footpath L across the field (150m). Turn L up the road (50m) then R on the footpath straight up the hillside (200m).

⑬ Don't turn R at the cross path but go on up (30m), round R and along the hillside above gardens (300m) then beside a field (200m).

⑭ Watch out for access R and go down the field (150m) then along the bottom to the road (100m).

⑮ Cross slightly L and follow the track opposite. When it bends R to the sheds (100m) continue ahead through the wood (100m) and turn L along the track skirting the base of the hill (500m). Just before the house, join the sunken path R. Go L to the drive (50m) and descend L to the *White Horse* (100m).

33 Dunsfold and Pockford

About 7½ km/4½ miles through woods and farmland; undulating; too muddy for winter walking; excellent for bluebells and other spring flowers.
OS maps: 1:25000 133 Haslemere +134 Crawley; 1:50000 186 Aldershot.

Start from Dunsfold, TQ 006 363, at the car park on the village green.

Linking walks 23✪ 24✪ 31☆ 32★

The Sun ☎ 01483 200242

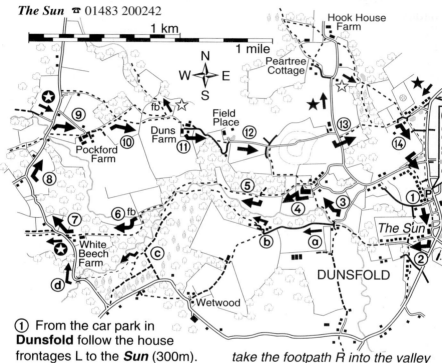

① From the car park in **Dunsfold** follow the house frontages L to the **Sun** (300m).

② Turn R along the lane after the pub. At the end continue on the path, then along Mill Lane (350m). Keep on down the track through the wood, over the bridge (250m) and on to the house L (150m).

ⓐ *A slightly longer alternative, too muddy in winter: Cross the drive and go straight on up the track beside the wood (450m).*

ⓑ *At the path junction just after the cottage turn R & L & R on the main track to the next cottage (100m). Just before the garden*

take the footpath R into the valley (600m). At a L bend in the stream join the forestry track and follow it R near the stream until it bends L up the valley side (700m).

ⓒ *Take the onward footpath up to the fork (100m) then the lesser path down R following the stream all the way to the lane (400m).*

ⓓ *Go over the bridge and up the lane to White Beech (400m). ↱⑦*

③ Cross the bridge R (20m) and take the footpath L beside the stream to the well then R up to **Dunsfold Church** (250m).

66

④ Walk through the churchyard, round the church (100m) and up R into the adjacent small field. Go L along the bottom edge (70m) and down through the wood (200m).

⑤ Join the cart track into the field and follow the edge of the wood R. When the narrow field bends R go straight over to the L corner, near the stream (300m), out over the bridge, through the wood (400m) and beside the next field (200m).

⑥ At the end turn L over the footbridge and climb out of the valley (100m). Keep on along the path to the lane at White Beech Farm (600m). ❍ Turn R.

⑦ Stay on the lane, over the hill and down to the junction (550m).

⑧ Carry on R down Vann Lane to the bridge just after Rosebank Cottage (300m).

⑨ Immediately over the bridge cross the field R to the corner near the barns of Pockford Farm (250m). (Alternatively stay on the lane (200m) and take the farm drive R (250m).) Follow the track past the buildings to the fields (100m). When it bends R keep on ahead along the edge (150m).

⑩ Half way along the small wood, L, join the crossing path ½R up the field (150m). Go through the hedge and on along the L edge of the next field (300m). ☆ The hedge curves up R to a barn and is joined by paths at the gap L.

⑪ Before the barn the path diverges L through the hedge to Duns Farm (50m). Walk down the track (L) between the buildings into the valley (200m) then up the other side. Keep on the track up round the hairpin bend (300m) or cut the corner up the steep field to the drive from Field Place.

⑫ Carry on along the drive over the rise (500m) and down to the lane (300m). ★

⑬ Just along the lane R (50m) enter the field on the other side. Follow the L boundary to the end (150m) and continue on the path down through the wood and up the other side (150m). Keep on along the R edge of the field and out on the track to the corner of the green at Dunsfold (150m).

⑭ Follow the R edge of the green round to the lane (450m). Cross it and carry on along the house frontages to the car park (200m).

The route crosses a Greensand fringe onto the Weald Clay - the underlying Cretaceous stratum which outcrops in the middle of the Weald. The ground is waterlogged much of the year and cleft by deep brooks. As little use can be made of the soil, this the most tree covered region of Britain. The paths indicate how difficult transport must have been before hard roads arrived. Despite the proximity of London the middle of the Weald has been one of the most isolated regions of England.

Weald Clay is a misleading geological name. The 400m stratum includes thin layers of sand which outcrop to form pockets of useful land. The Horsham sandstone and Sussex marble are part of it further south. The sandstone is split into Horsham slabs - the massive uneven slates used in roofs around Horsham and to a lesser extent in Surrey. The clay itself was used for brick making, as at Smithbrook Kilns.

When this was the main centre of iron making in Roman and medieval times, the ore was siderite nodules dug out of the clay. Names like Minepit Copse and Furnace Place are a legacy of the industry. The woods were given over to coppicing for charcoal production.

34 Bramley and Lordshill

About 8½ km/5¼ miles mainly over farmland but with a long stretch of road through the village centres; long climbs but not very steep and many stiles; fairly shady. OS maps: 1:25000 145 Guildford; 1:50000 186 Aldershot.

Start from the middle of Bramley, TQ 009 448. There is parking behind the shops near the Catholic Church and around the Village Hall in Hall Road.

Linking walks   9✿   11✦   27✳   28✳   35✿   ㉜ ✳

The Grantley Arms ☎ 01483 893351
The Wheatsheaf ☎ 01483 892722
The Jolly Farmer ☎ 01483 893355

✿① From **Bramley** crossroads walk along Station Road past the ex-railway station, L (200m), and over **Cranleigh Water** (300m). ✦

② At the junction keep on round the bend, past an old house, Green Place, and along The Street to the Pepper Pot and *Grantley Arms* in the middle of **Wonersh** (500m).

③ Start along the road L towards Guildford (200m) but turn off R at the green and keep to the R edge to the next road (150m). A little R (30m) cross into the track by the old house, Woodyers. Continue on the footpath between fields up **Barnett Hill** past the eponymous house to the next lane (1000m).

④ Don't join the lane but turn back R down the track. Follow the track around outside the L edge of the cemetery. If very muddy walk on top of the R bank (400m). ✳

⑤ Opposite Lyne's Farm turn R on the path down the valley. Pass through small fields and a garden (450m) and on (200m). After the next house continue ahead on the tarmac drive but when it curves R (350m) keep on ahead along the footpath which joins the main road dangerously (100m). ✿

⑥ Cross the road into the drive slightly R. Carry on past the **Wonersh Mill** house (350m) to the corner of the wall L (100m).

⑦ Go L down over the stream and on along the track. Look over the wall into the garden (200m). At the lane go R and keep on to the green at Lordshill (700m).

⑧ Return a few steps and take the tarmac drive to Westland Farm (150m). Skirt the buildings and carry on along the track (450m) ultimately turning L then R over Cranleigh Water and the **Junction Canal**. Pass under the Downs Link path (on the disused embankment of the **Horsham Railway**) up to the road (300m).

⑨ Follow the pavement L past farm buildings (300m). Just round the curve cross to the 1st tarmac drive opposite and ascend past Birtley House and on (550m). ✳

⑩ Before the farm buildings turn R up the drive (300m).

⑪ Just before the house take the path R under the trees then between fields to Hurst Hill Farm (700m) and on through the woods down to Bramley (700m).

⑫ At the end of the path keep on along the road ahead to the bend (100m) then between the houses (100m) and on along the main road past the *Wheatsheaf*, *Jolly Farmer* and church to the crossroads (400m).

The River Wey appears to have made its original channel through Bramley for the hills are the sides of a great valley aligned with the notch where the main river cuts through the North Downs at Guildford. The rivulet in the valley is called the Bramley Stream or Cranleigh Water. It joins the present Wey at Shalford just before the Tilling Bourne flows into the river.

The Wey starts as two major tributaries which rise near Alton and Churt, each called Wey. They join at Tilford and flow to the Thames at Weybridge.

The streams around Dunsfold and Chiddingfold flow the other way. They are headwaters of the Arun which they enter via the Loxford Stream. The Arun rises near Horsham and flows into the English Channel at Littlehampton.

35 Shamley Green to Daneshill

About 6½ km/4 miles: a Greensand Way walk across the great Wey valley mainly through arable farmland. OS maps: 1:25000 145 Guildford; 1:50000 186 Aldershot.

Start from Shamley Green, TQ 032 438 in Woodhill Lane off the crossroads. Do not park near the cricket green if play may start while you are away.

Linking walks   27✿   28★   34✿   36✿   37✧   ㉜✦   ㉝✦

The Bricklayers Arms ☎ 01483 898377
The Red Lion ☎ 01483 892202

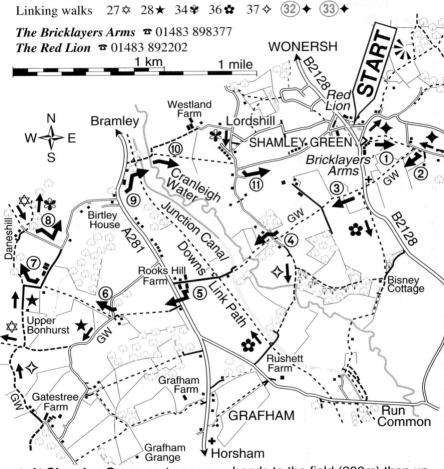

✦ At **Shamley Green** make your way to the corner of the green next to the ***Bricklayers' Arms***.

① Just before the pub take the track L from the main road (50m) and turn into the footpath between the drives before the Malt House. Follow the path around several bends to the field (200m) then up beside the hedge (200m).

② Turn R on the path across the top of the field. The route now follows the **Greensand Way**. Carry straight on to the church and cross the road into the church car park (450m). ✿

70

③ Keep on ahead between fields, over a farm track (300m) and down to a tarmac drive (400m). ✧

④ Find the onward path slightly R and continue in the same direction down to the stream, **Cranleigh Water** (400m). Cross the bridge and follow the R boundary to the top of the field (on the line of the **Junction Canal**)(300m). Pass out along the cart track, over the old **Horsham Railway** bridge (Downs Link path underneath) and past the barns of Rooks Hill Farm to the main road (400m).

⑤ Walk along the pavement L until just before the next house on the other side (150m) then cross into track beside it and keep on up the field and around the garden hedge to the lane (450m). The Greensand Way continues up the lane but you don't. ★

⑥ Find the footpath up the bank, opposite, and follow it into the field and on up the L boundary beside the wood (300m). At the top, spy out the stiles ahead and keep on in the same direction down over a little valley and up R of the farm house (200m).

⑦ On the farm track go L to the house (50m), round the bend and uphill (100m). ✿ At the next bend turn R up the bridleway under the trees (350m) and keep on slightly R at the cart track (100m). ❀

⑧ At the junction near the house, Daneshill, turn R down the drive to the farm track (300m) then L down to the main road (600m).

⑨ Cross to the pavement. Follow the road L past Birtley Courtyard (300m) and take the track down R under the footbridge of the Downs Link path and over the Junction Canal and Cranleigh Water up to the edge of the fields (250m).

⑩ Don't turn L with the track but climb to the fields and go straight on to the next lane (600m).

⑪ Go R on the lane (50m), round the L bend and on all the way to Shamley Green (800m).

Trig points give joy to walkers and status to hills. They were built for the third triangulation of Great Britain which the Ordnance Survey started in 1936 and became redundant in 1990 when global positioning technology was judged to

be as accurate as traditional survey methods. In all, 6500 were built. The English ones are mostly tapered square pillars of local stone or concrete. The fundamental mark is a brass stud set in a concrete block a metre below the pillar and there is another in the bottom of the pillar. The brass spider on top is for fixing instruments.

In triangulation, angles from two points, accurately sighted on a third, allow its position to be calculated by trigonometry, hence trigonometric survey and trig point. Sightings were made at night using lamps. In the 1950s trig points were painted white for aerial surveying.

Gibbet Hill (Hindhead) trig point (1938) was used in the primary triangulation over distances of 50km/30 miles. Hydon's Ball trig point was secondary with triangles of 8km/5 miles. The first triangulation started in 1784 from a base line which now ends in Heathrow.

Ordnance Survey - map makers to Britain since 1791 T Owen & E Pilbeam OS 1992

36 Shamley Green and Whipley

9 km/5¾ miles or 11km/7 miles; undulating farmland. OS maps: 1:25000 145+134; 1:50000 186 Aldershot.

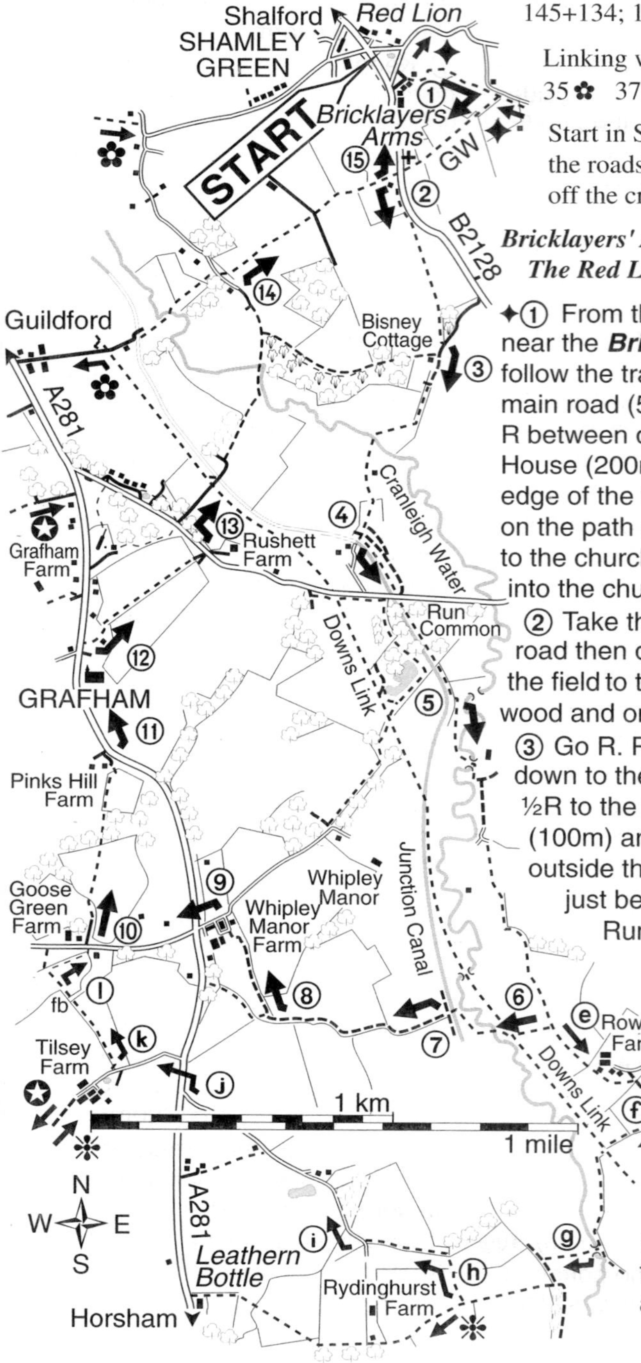

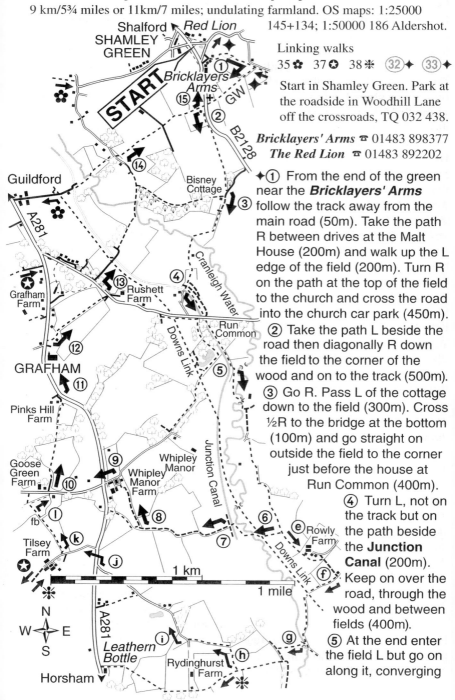

Linking walks
35✿ 37✪ 38✻ (32)✦ (33)✦

Start in Shamley Green. Park at the roadside in Woodhill Lane off the crossroads, TQ 032 438.

Bricklayers' Arms ☎ 01483 898377
The Red Lion ☎ 01483 892202

✦① From the end of the green near the ***Bricklayers' Arms*** follow the track away from the main road (50m). Take the path R between drives at the Malt House (200m) and walk up the L edge of the field (200m). Turn R on the path at the top of the field to the church and cross the road into the church car park (450m).

② Take the path L beside the road then diagonally R down the field to the corner of the wood and on to the track (500m).

③ Go R. Pass L of the cottage down to the field (300m). Cross ½R to the bridge at the bottom (100m) and go straight on outside the field to the corner just before the house at Run Common (400m).

④ Turn L, not on the track but on the path beside the **Junction Canal** (200m). Keep on over the road, through the wood and between fields (400m).

⑤ At the end enter the field L but go on along it, converging on the stream below, **Cranleigh Water**. Follow the bank round towards East Whipley farmhouse. Cross the stock bridge and go R to the gate (40m). Outside, follow the track R, along the valleyside, through the fields. In the 2nd field take a few steps L on the concrete. In the 3rd follow the L hedge up a little way, then go on as before to the side path down R, 200m before Rowly Farm (900m).

ⓔ *Longer version: Stay on the track up to Rowley Farm and pass between the houses and gardens. At the end turn L round the edge of the field (350m) then R along the track to the next house (150m).*

ⓕ *Enter the field R and go down the L edges (200m). Cross the Downs Link path and carry on round L to the footbridge R (350m).*

ⓖ *Cross the stream and go on between fields (200m) then L on the track (100m). At the junction go R on the track then path to the end of the long field R (300m).* ✳

ⓗ *Turn R on the side path (150m). When it ends in a field, follow the hedge L to the farm drive (300m).*

ⓘ *Walk along the drive R to the next houses (350m) then on along the lane to the main road (500m).*

ⓙ *Follow the road R (100m) then turn L up to Tilsey Farm (250m).* ✪

ⓚ *Just before the farm buildings turn back R into the field and follow the L edge to the end (300m). Cross the bridge and go on ahead beside the hedge then over to the stile (100m).*

ⓛ *Go R along the edge of the field & out at the gate (150m).* ➜⑩

⑥ Turn R down to the bottom of the field. Cross the Downs Link path (150m) then the stream (100m) and continue R through the valley and over the Junction Canal to the farm tracks (100m).

⑦ Keep on up the track ahead beside L boundaries (600m).

⑧ At the top, follow the bend in the track towards Whipley Manor Farm and pass between the buildings to the main drive (450m).

⑨ Walk out of the farm L and cross the main road (100m). Carry on along the lane (350m).

⑩ Take the track R of Goose Green Farm into the field and up the R boundary (150m). Cross into the field R and go straight up to the middle of the top boundary (150m) then out through the wood (100m) and along the L edge of the next field (150m). Just past the house join the drive L and go down to the road (70m). Cross.

⑪ Follow the road L to Grafham Church (200m) and on (100m).

⑫ Just after the Grange drive L turn R on the narrow path under trees to the field (100m). Follow the R edge to the far end (400m).

⑬ Go L on the lane (150m) and turn along the next track R ✿ over the **Horsham Railway** bridge and on into the field (300m). When the track bends L carry on ahead near the edge then straight down to the stream (300m) and along the bank (100m). Cross the footbridge and keep on up the path then along the track to the house (300m).

⑭ Continue on the tarmac drive (70m) then take the side path R up between the fields all the way to the church car park (650m).

⑮ Walk along the lane L into Shamley Green (300m).

37 Grafham and Wintershall

About 7½ km/4¾ miles and two 1 km/¾ mile extensions; undulating farmland.
OS maps: 1:25000 145 Guildford +134 Crawley; 1:50000 186 Aldershot.

Start from Rushett Common, TQ 022 423; park in one of the rough laybys on
the minor road close to junction with the A281. No pub.

Linking walks 27✦ 28✪
29❖ 35✧ 36✪ 38✳

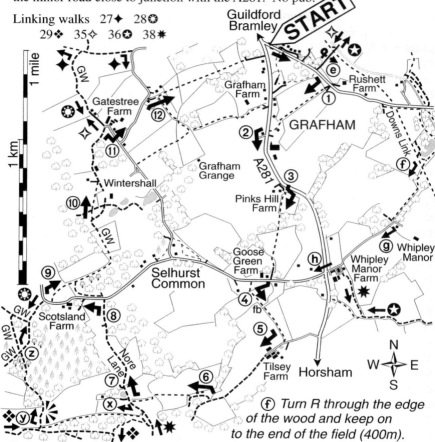

*(f) Turn R through the edge
of the wood and keep on
to the end of the field (400m).*

*(g) At the end go L on the cart
track (20m) then R up the tarmac
drive R to Whipley Manor Farm ✳
and out of the gateway (550m).*

*(h) Cross the main road and go on
along the lane to Goose Green
Farm house (350m). ✦④*

From your parking place start
along the minor road away from
the junction past the houses L. ✪

*(e) Extension: After the pond carry
on (100m) and take the 2nd track L
(200m). Just over the **Horsham
Railway** bridge, descend L to the
Downs Link path. Walk under the
bridge and on (SE), under a road
(500m) to the next crossing footpath (450m) just after a cart track.*

① After the pond carry on along
the road (250m) and turn R on the
footpath at the end of the 1st field,
opposite the track from the farm.

Follow the L edge to the far end (400m) and pass out between gardens to the main road (100m).

② Go L along the pavement past Grafham Church and on (300m).

③ At the top of the hill cross to the drives and go L to Pinks Hill Farm (70m). Enter the field then pass R in front of the house and on along the R boundary (150m). Go on through the wood (100m) then ½R down the next field to the R edge before it curves away R (200m). Find the crossing point to the field R and walk down the L edge and out on the track through the trees to the lane at Goose Green Farm house (150m). ✳

④ Opposite the house, go round the hedge corner to the gate into the field. Follow the R edge as far as the stile R (150m) then cross the field L to the protruding corner. Keep on ahead along the hedge (100m), over the footbridge and up the R side of the next field (300m).

⑤ At the end join the tarmac drive and go up between the barns of Tilsey Farm and out on the gravel track until it meets the wood converging from R (650m).

⑥ Take the branch track R into the wood round past the buildings. When it bends L (150m) go out of the corner into the field R and straight up, aiming for the middle of the top edge (200m). Pass through the gap to the field above, then L up into the adjacent field (50m) and follow the R edge out to the track (150m). ❖ ⇘

ⓧ *Hilly extension: Turn L up the sunken track (130m). On the bend climb the stepped path R. Turn R and go up beside the field (700m).*

ⓨ *At the top join the horse track and go R up the ridge between the fields (150m) then through the wood past a field corner (200m) down to the cross track (200m).* ⊙

ⓩ *Turn R and follow the track all the way down to the lane (400m). Down the lane R (40m), join the footpath on the other side.* →⑨

⑦ Follow the track R over the rise and down to the lane (700m).

⑧ Walk up the lane (L) over the ridge and down past Scotsland Farm (300m) and on (50m) to the footpath R before the bend. ⊙

⑨ Follow the footpath round R below the hillside field at the edge of the wood then L into the field (500m). Go on across the field parallel with the top edge (200m).

⑩ Take the track out at the other side over the little valley but when it bends R keep ahead across another track (150m) then ½R over the grass past the corner of the **Wintershall** gardens down to the boundary track before the cottage (200m). Continue along the track which curves R to Gatestree Farm (450m). ✦❖

⑪ Turn R along the lane (150m) and L at the next junction. Walk down past the next house (350m).

⑫ Turn in R beside the house on the track to the fields (100m). Go straight over two narrow fields (200m) and on down the middle of the long one (usually no visible path). Pass close to the bulges in the wood R and aim for the gateway at the bottom edge, 50m from the R corner (400m). Go out on the track (150m) then cross the main road and the corner of the Common to your parking place.

38 Whipley and Smithbrook

About 8 km/5 miles but can be varied, in farmland, undulating.
OS maps: 1:25000 145 Guildford +134 Crawley; 1:50000 186 Aldershot.

Linking walks   29✳   32✸   36✳   37✳

Start near the *Leathern Bottle*, TQ 026 395; park on the verge at the footpath.

The Leathern Bottle 01483 274117   ***Smithbrook Kilns*** cafe 01483 274117

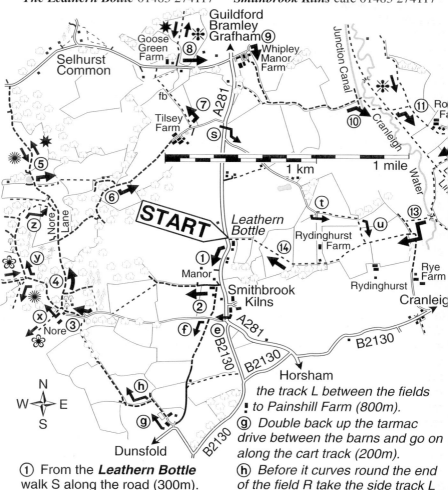

① From the **Leathern Bottle**
walk S along the road (300m).

ⓔ *Summer extension of 1¼ km/*
¾ mile: Keep on beside the road
past the Smithbrook Kilns craft
centre to the road junction (200m).

ⓕ *Just before it, turn R up the*
drive (100m). After the 1st field take

the track L between the fields
to Painshill Farm (800m).

ⓖ *Double back up the tarmac*
drive between the barns and go on
along the cart track (200m).

ⓗ *Before it curves round the end*
of the field R take the side track L
over the rise and down until it splits
to 4 fields (200m). Turn R on the
track up the R boundary and go on
up the top field. Watch out for the
path out R under the trees. Follow
it to the lane (700m). ➜**③**

② Turn R on the track at the drive of Smithbrook Cottage. Carry on at the R edge of the fields to the entrance to the top field (400m) then go ½L up the middle of the field to the top L corner. The path is usually invisible (350m). Join the lane and walk up the hill R past the drive of The Pheasantry to the gateway of Nore (200m).

③ Fork R up the rough track until it bends L (100m). ✳

ⓧ *Hilly extension of 500m with fine views: Stay on the track round L & R bends and up steeply to the path junction on the ridge (400m).*

ⓨ *Take the track up R to the end of the ridge (450m).*

ⓩ *Carry on off the end, down R (300m). At the bottom go L (50m) then down the stepped path R to the track and L (150m).* ➔⑤

④ Don't go round the bend but ahead through the wood. Ignore a side track R into fields (500m) and carry on over another rise to the dip with the pond (450m). ✳

⑤ Just before the pond (which dries), turn R over the field, next to (R of) the hedge (150m). At the corner, drop to the adjacent field L and pass through the opening into the field below R (50m). Go down the field converging on the R side to the protruding corner of the wood (200m). In the wood join the track L past the buildings & round R to a major farm track (150m).

⑥ Follow the track L to and through Tilsey Farm (650m).

ⓢⓣⓤ *Short cut: See map.*

⑦ Just after the barns and pond R, enter the field L and follow the L boundary to the end (300m). Cross the footbridge ahead and keep on beside the hedge until it bends L then cross the field to the stile, slightly L (100m). If the way out is blocked, go R along the edge and out at the gate opposite Goose Green Farm (150m). ✳

⑧ Walk along the lane R (350m). Cross the main road and follow the drive, opposite, into Whipley Manor Farm (100m).

⑨ Take the 3rd tarmac side road between the barn and house and go on along the track which bends L then follows the field boundaries (450m). Carry on round the L bend and down through the fields beside the hedge (600m).

⑩ At the end cross the **Junction Canal** footbridge and follow the path R through the valley, over **Cranleigh Water** and up (250m). Cross the Downs Link path and keep on ahead up the field (150m).

⑪ At the top turn R on the South Wey path to Rowly Farm (200m). Pass between the houses and gardens. At the end follow the L bend round the edge of the field (200m) then turn R along the track to the next house (150m).

⑫ Enter the field R and go down the L edges (200m). Cross the Downs Link path and carry on round L to the footbridge R (350m).

⑬ Go over the stream and on between fields (200m) then L to the junction (100m). Turn R on the track and continue on the footpath between fields, past a side path R (300m) and on. Cross the top end of a field. Pass L of the farmhouse and through the next field (500m).

⑭ Look ahead to the *Leathern Bottle* and follow the line of stiles ½R then up to the pub (500m).

Albury was the Domesday Book manor ELDEBERIE. It already had a church and mill. The estate stayed in the d'Abernon family for 5 centuries but has passed through many families since. The medieval village was near the old church but in the 18th century pressure was put on villagers to move to the present site and Henry Drummond, a 19th century owner, built the new village church in 1842. Notable residents have been Malthus the political economist, Anthony Devis the painter and Martin Tupper the writer. The estate came to the Dukes of Northumberland through the marriage of Drummond's daughter.

Albury - a short guide to the parish 1998 24pp

Barnett Hill house was built about 1905 in Queen Anne style by a London businessman, Frank Cook. His widow gave it to the Red Cross in 1944. It had already been used as a convalescent hospital and went on to become the national training centre, archive and conference centre of the Red Cross.

Binscombe has several old houses and the air of an ancient settlement. The area was one of the ancient tithings of Godalming. The housing developments which have joined it to Farncombe have brought to light much broken pottery of the Roman period. *Bin* usually derives from bean.

Blackheath was the name of the Domesday Book hundred that included Bramley, Chilworth, Shalford, etc. The men of the hundred would probably have met and held courts in the open on the heath. The village lies in the midst of the Common, 108 hectares, managed by Waverley BC for recreation and conservation. The Canadian army enclosed it as a camp in World War II and ended the grazing; it had been used for army training for the Napoleonic wars and in Victorian times. *The Villagers* was originally *The Volunteer Arms*.

Bramley must have been a great Saxon estate probably including Hascombe, Dunsfold, Alfold and Cranleigh, for the Domesday Book lists no other place between BRVNLEI and the Sussex border and it had three churches and five mills. William the Conqueror gave it to his half brother Odo, the Bishop of Bayeux. Bramley Mill is a 17th century building; it operated until 1935. A railway platform is retained with fervour despite the absence of trains & rails.

Bramley & Grafham - a short history Bramley Village Society 1977 47pp

Bramley Church, Holy Trinity, is probably on the site of one of the Domesday Book churches but the nave is Victorian. The aisles are almost as large as the nave. The oldest fabric extant is the west door arch (inside the porch) which is probably Norman. The chancel dates from around 1210.

Catteshall Manor house was the headquarters of the Pitman organisation 1952-96. It appears to be a large Victorian house but has a 17th century core and remnants of the structure of Henry I's time when he detached Catteshall from the large royal manor of Godalming for his retainer Dyvus Purcell. The house at the bottom of the hill (sometime *The Ram* pub), is ancient, originally a hall house ie with a central roof-high room containing a hearth but no chimney. It took its name from the hydraulic ram pump (in box opposite) installed in the 1920s by John Blake Ltd to push water up to Unsted Park.

Catteshall Mill was probably one of the three Domesday Book mills of Godalming; in 1141 it was part of a grant to Reading Abbey. Its earliest recorded uses were as a fulling mill and a corn mill. The rent in 1509 was 43 shillings and 10 sticks of eels! By 1661 it was a paper mill and in 1885 one of the first to use wood pulp. A sales poster of 1906 says it produced 80 tons of paper per week. The water wheels were replaced with a turbine in 1869 which last rotated in 1960. This was the largest known Fournyron turbine (37 kW); there is a model of it in Godalming museum.

Catteshall Mill   Alan & Glenys Crocker Surrey Arch Soc Research Vol 8 1981 64pp

Chantries Hill is a Greensand ridge with thin seams of Bargate stone which give greater fertility and permit grassland instead of heath in the Five Fields. It was given to Holy Trinity Church, Guildford in 1486 by Henry Norbrigge (mayor, d.1512; there is a brass plate to him near George Abbott's tomb). The rent or produce of a chantry paid a church for prayers for the soul of the donor or others. Usually it funded a church school whose pupils chanted the prayers. Chantries were dissolved soon after the monasteries by Acts of 1545 & 1547.

Chiddingfold is a fine example of nuclear village with church, inn and pond clustered at the corner of the green and the old houses round it. *The Crown* is partly 14th century and has probably been an inn throughout. Despite its evident antiquity Chiddingfold is not a Domesday Book village, its tax being lumped with Godalming's at that time. The earliest mention of *Chedelingefelt* is in a charter of about 1130. It became a market town by charter of Edward I in 1300 when it was the main centre of glass production and part of the great iron making region. On local maps, *glasshouse* denotes the site of an ancient glassworks. About 40 are known locally, ten of them in the parish. Ancient records of churches elsewhere show orders for Chiddingfold glass. The village church, St Mary, has lancet windows, pillars and chancel arch in Early English style dating from soon after 1200. The nave roof was raised around 1450 on extended pillars. The lych gate with its coffin table and Horsham slabs was added in 1888 and restored in 1980.

Chiddingfold - the village and history of the Parish Church of St Mary H R H White 1999 44pp

Chilworth is CELEORDE in the Domesday Book, a small manor with a mill, owned by Bishop Odo of Bayeux. The present manor house is a 17th century re-build by Vincent Randyll, owner of manor and gunpowder mills, 1653-73, who sold up to the Duchess of Marlborough after the South Sea Bubble.

Chinthurst Hill was bought by SCC as public open space in 1961 to forestall building. The tower is a folly put up in 1936 when the Chinthurst estate was part of Lord Inchcape's property. An ancient boundary mound crosses the hill close to the modern Waverley/Guildford border. The eponymous house, 1895, was Lutyen's first large commission. It is now subdivided.

Compton is ancient. There was a Roman house but the name first appears in writing in 727 when 4 hides of Compton were gifted to Chertsey Abbey. It is CONTONE in the Domesday Book, a manor of 14 hides owned by Edward the Confessor and tenanted by Brixi. In King John's time it was split into the Manors of Down (north of the Hog's Back), Polsted, Westbury, Eastbury and Field Place, still represented by large houses of these names. The *Harrow Inn* has been licensed since at least 1780. White Hart Cottage is a 15th century house; it was a pub (before 1780) and may have been the church ale house.

The History of Compton in Surrey Lady C Boston Compton Parochial Council 1987 247pp

Compton Church, St Nicholas, has a Saxon tower. The nave walls were replaced by hard chalk pillars when the aisles were added about 1160. The Norman doorway (inside the porch), font, lozenge mural over the chancel arch and coloured glass in the east window are all 12th century work. The chapel above the sanctuary is very unusual and its wooden guard rail exceedingly old. A Crusader graffito is scratched on the south side of the chancel arch.

Cosford Mill has the oldest machinery in Surrey and parts of the building are 15th century. It closed in the 1890s. The wheel was taken for iron in WWII.

Cranleigh Water is a small river in an immense valley which provides fine views from its sides, the hills above Shamley Green and Hascombe. It is aligned with the Guildford notch in the North Downs so must be regarded as the original River Wey though it is smaller than the present tributaries.

Cutt Mill is mentioned in a medieval document in 1273 when it was given in a marriage settlement by John le Cotte to John le Paumer. The only remains of the mill, which functioned until the 1930s, are the pillars and shed in front of the house. The present house is the mill cottage. The millpond is probably medieval in origin but the ponds forming a ladder a mile up the valley are Repton's work of the 1800s when he landscaped Hampton Park.

The **Devil's Punch Bowl** first appears in name in Rocque's *Map of the County of Surrey* of 1765. Its old name was Highcombe or Haccombe or, in a charter of 909, Hegcumbe which may derive from hay-growing where the bottom has cut down to the Atherfield Clay. From inside it appears to be surrounded by hills but it is a very large coomb set in the side of one - Gibbet Hill. The clay raises the water table into the sides. The several springs easily sap the Hythe beds which are mainly unlithified sands but the sides remain steep because of low rainfall and the sand causes absorption rather than run-off.

Dunsfold is part of the greatest concentration of *fold* names in Britain, from the Saxon *falod*, implying a place of sheep folding. It was *Duntesfold* when first written in an Assize Roll of 1241; Dunt was a Saxon personal name. Folds were fields used in winter; for most of the year the sheep would have been led off along moltways to wander on the heaths.

Dunsfold Church, St Mary & All the Saints, is almost in its original form of around 1260-1320 when Early English was becoming Decorated. In Victorian times the chancel arch was raised, the east window truncated and the west window rebuilt. Points of interest: the cruciform plan unusual for a small village church, very ancient pews, three plug holes for floor washing visible externally (one in the west wall) and the elaborate sedilia.

Dunsfold airfield assembled jet fighters until 2001. It is not much seen from the ground but aircraft sometimes obtrude. It was constructed in 20 weeks by Canadian Army Engineers in 1942 as a Royal Canadian Air Force base in the build up to D-Day. It started with Mustangs, which shot up trains in France, and went on to have Mitchell bombers. After the war in 1946 it was loaned to Skyways Ltd whose Skymasters and Dakotas made 2749 flights in the Berlin Airlift (1948-49). Hawker took over in 1951, for testing prototypes and assembling the Sea Hawk, Hunter, Folland Gnat, Hawk and Harrier.

Dunsfold, Surrey's most secret airfield Paul McCue 1992 Air Research Publications 297pp

Eashing is listed as Æscengum in Alfred the Great's will drafted around 885 - a bequest to his nephew Ædhelm. It is Escingum in the *Burhal Hidage* written about 915. This was crown land and approximately equidistant from London, Winchester and the sea. Lower Eashing was a farming hamlet. *Tankards*, built about 1700, was perhaps a farm manager's house. The block of offices, half on the island, replaced Eashing Mill in 1998. This may have been one of the three Domesday Book mills of Godalming. It was sold as a corn mill in 1658 but converted to paper making in the 1830s. By 1865 its 98 employees made 10 tons of paper per week for *The Times* and other newspapers. Latterly it was a flock mill then became an engineering works. The 13th century Eashing bridges are of Bargate Sandstone and similar to the Wey bridges at Tilford, Waverley, Elstead and Unsted, generally attributed to the monks of Waverley.

Elstead would have been in existence at the time of the Domesday Book but it is not listed because its data was lumped in with the rest of the great manor of Farnham. The name is first documented in the founding charter of Waverley Abbey in 1128 when of two acres of HELESTED were donated by the Bishop of Winchester. The old houses of the village are the 16th century *Peace Haven* and *Lilac Cottage* in Milford Road, *Old Farmhouse* in Farnham Road and *Domford* in Thursley Road. The forge at the green dates from 1686. Polshott Manor was the Stovold family farmhouse for 400 years from the 15th century but has not been a working farm since 1920. *Brookside* started as a small 16th century cottage but has grown. Peter Sellers (1959) and Ringo Starr lived there. Elstead Bridge was re-built in the 16th century and resembles the bridges attributed to the Waverley monks. The second lane was added in WWII.

Elstead then and now Gillian Drew 2001 81pp

Elstead Church, St James, was a chapel of Farnham by 1291 but building styles suggests it was started in the middle of the 12th century. Built of chalk and bargate, the 14th century parts still visible are the blocked doorway in the chancel, the pointed chancel arch and the middle window in the north wall.

Elstead Mill is a restaurant. The building dates from about 1800 but is likely to be on the site of one of the six Domesday Book mills of Farnham. When work ceased in 1881 it was making worsted fringes. In the 17th century it had been a corn, malt and fulling mill and the previous building was erected in 1648. Helstede mill was entered at 10s 3d in a rent roll of 1208.

Enton was part of the Rectory manor of Godalming owned by Flambard. He was the chief adviser of William Rufus but lost his land when the fatal arrow brought brother Henry to power. Enton Mill survives incorporated into a house. It probably originated in the 15th century; milling ceased in 1899.

The **Ford Farm** fish ponds are used for producing trout to stock angling ponds on the Albury estate and at Syon House - for the same owner.

Gatwick is a fairly common name from the Saxon for goat place or farm. This would be consistent with the surrounding heath.

Gibbet Hill has a trig point at 272.85m/895', making it the second highest hill in Surrey. The Celtic Cross was set up in 1851 on the command of Lord Chief Justice Earle on the site of the gibbet when it finally fell. The murderers of the unknown sailor were executed on this gibbet in 1787. Their bodies were tarred for preservation and rehung on chains until they disintegrated

POST OBITUM SALUS   After death, salvation   IN OBITU PAX   In death, peace
POST TENEBRAS LUX   After darkness, light   IN LUCE SPES   In light, hope

The track skirting the northern edge of the top is the old Portsmouth road. The sailor's stone 100m down to the west marks the place where the sailor's body was found in 1786; Dickens has Nicholas Nickleby reading the inscription to Smike as they walk to Portsmouth. The present main road arrived in 1826.

Godalming Hundred appears as a bequest in the will of Alfred the Great, drafted around 885. The charter for a market was given by Edward I in 1300. Borough status was granted by Elizabeth I in 1574 and held until 1974 when the town was subsumed into Waverley. The coat-of-arms shows a woolsack: Godalming was a centre for sheep rearing, weaving, fulling and dyeing, in medieval times, with power provided by the Rivers Wey and Ock. High Street was the London to Portsmouth road with several coaching inns. The *Kings Arms* still looks the part; Peter the Great stayed there in 1698. The *Red Lion*'s public bar was the old Godalming Grammar School. Prisoners on the way to Portsmouth for transportation were incarcerated at this inn. The Pepperpot is the old Townhall. It replaced the medieval Hundred House (court and office) on the same site in 1814. The town became a terminus on the LSWR branch line from Woking in 1849 but the present station opened in 1859 when the line was extended to Havant to connect with Portsmouth.

Godalming - a Short History John Janaway 1993 Ammonite Books 77pp.

Godalming Church, SS Peter & Paul, was restored by Gilbert Scott in 1879. It is a well preserved large medieval church built on the original Saxon walls with some 9th century carved stones. The lead sheathed spire is 14th century.

The **Godalming Navigation** reached Godalming in 1763, an extension of the Wey Navigation from Guildford, and like it, is a mixture of improved river bed and cuts. It rises 10m/32 feet from Guildford with four locks: Millmead, St Catherine's, Unsted and Catteshall. It carried freight until the wharfs closed in 1925. In 1968 the commissioners gave it to Guildford Corporation who off-loaded it onto the National Trust.

Gosden Common was the venue for a cricket match reported in the *Reading Mercury* in 1745 which appears to be the first recorded women's match; see the plaque on the pavilion. The Bramley maidens scored 119 notches and the Hamble*t*on maidens, 127; lbw may have been a problem. Gosden House, now a school was Osbert Sitwell's grandmother's and appears to appear in his work.

The Greensand Way, officially opened in 1980, is a 110 mile path from Haslemere, Surrey to Hamstreet, Kent.

Hambledon is a Domesday Book village. No church was recorded in the Domesday Book but tax documents show there was a church by 1291. The present building was erected in 1846 but has memorials from earlier churches. Court Farm, the 17th century house next door, was the Manor House which held Court Leet and Court Baron. The kiln opposite the church was for chalk lime to be spread on the fields. *The Merry Harriers* is an 18th century house.

Hambledon Hurst has very fine forest oaks on Wealden Clay. It typifies the terrain which gave the Weald its name- Saxon for forest - and which made penetration of the country difficult before hard roads were built. The toll road, now the A283, was built 1780-1790 and raised in 1820.

Hammer ponds powered mills for the hammers and bellows of furnaces and forges. Thursley had three hammer mills, two of them beside the Common. Lower Hammer Pond remains; the site of Upper Hammer Pond is under the A3. The earliest record is a lease from the Mores of Loseley in 1625 and pig iron was still arriving for forging in 1767. It is unlikely smelting was carried out; the Wealden iron industry was in its final phase when work spread into Surrey and no slag has been found. Lower Hammer Mill was converted to a silk mill for which there are records early in the 19th century.

Hascombe is not a Domesday Book manor but appears to have been cut off from Bramley around 1300. Hascombe Place Farm (17th century) was the manor house. At the village fountain local people still bottle their own free mineral water. The church, St Peter, is Victorian Gothic, built of Bargate in 1864, incorporating memorials, font and screen from the previous churches. The painting of the chancel is unusual. The advowson goes back to 1305.

Hascombe Court is an Edwardian house designed by J D Coleridge in the vernacular revival style promoted by Lutyens.

Hascombe Hill or Hascombe High Beech, 624ft/190m, has an Iron Age fort on top and, during the Napoleonic Wars, had one of the shutter signalling stations in the chain from the Admiralty to Portsmouth.

Hindhead has grown up on the boundaries of Thursley, Frensham and Haslemere parishes and extends into Hampshire. In the middle of the 19th century there were three cottages and an inn, *The Royal Huts*. It appears to have grown solely to serve the London to Portsmouth Road. Conan Doyle built the house *Undershaw*. The *Devil's Punchbowl* Hotel was built as a country house by the Hon Rollo Russell, son of Lord John.

The **Hog's Back** is the part of the North Downs where the bending of the strata is most extreme - the bedding in one of the chalk pits has a dip of 60°. The name first appears in a letter of 1802 quoted by Mowbray Howard in *The Longs of Jamaica and Hampton Lodge*. Gilbert White was still calling it Guildown in his diary in 1797. The road on top may be the oldest in England.

The **Horsham Railway** line from Guildford, opened in 1865 and closed in 1965. It began the demise of the Wey Navigation and Junction Canal and suffered the axe of the Dr Beeching cuts in 1965. It is now the route of the Downs Link path which goes under or over the bridges.

Hurtmore is mentioned in the Domesday Book, 1086, as HORMERA. It was a manor of 15 hides and one mill owned by Edward the Confessor but, after the conquest, given to Walter, Son of Othere. Many local place names include *priory* because from 1259 until the dissolution the manor was owned by the Priory of Newark (near Woking), though leased to farmers.

Hydon's Ball may owe its name to a signalling station with a ball. It is an outlier of the Folkstone sands on Bargate beds so has heath on top and fields below. The trig point is at 178.82m/587'. The reservoir in the hilltop serves Chiddingfold, Dunsfold and Hambledon and receives water from Greensand boreholes. To the west, the distant, asymmetric hill is Blackdown, the highest hill in Sussex. The knobbly peak to the right of it is Gibbet Hill above Hindhead. On the opposite side the North Downs are seen. The granite seat marks the gift of the land to the National Trust as a memorial to Octavia Hill.

Octavia Hill, 1838-1912, was a co-founder of the National Trust. She was the offspring of reformer parents and the NT was the outcome of the idealism and philanthropy stirred up by industrialization and urbanisation. The founders met through participation in the Commons Preservation Society (opposing illegal encroachment) and the Kyrle Society (which improved urban areas by planting). Robert Hunter drafted the constitution and legislation, Hardwicke Rawnsley had the contacts from his many campaigns and Octavia Hill was the indefatigable workhorse. Their ultimate solution was to own places worthy of preservation and the *National Trust for Places of Historic Interest or Natural Beauty* was registered under the Companies Act in 1895. Most social reforms of the age became the welfare state but the NT continues more or less as it started. It now controls more than ½m acres, 230 houses and 130 gardens.

The **Junction Canal** linked the thriving Arun and Wey Navigations in 1816. Much of it is now dry and some of it has been filled in. It was conceived at the time of the Napoleonic Wars and promoted as a way of avoiding French privateers on the sea route between London and Portsmouth. The Arun Navigation reached Newbridge in 1787. The Wey Navigation reached Guildford in 1653. Both had been successful but the Junction Canal across the Weald came too late and leaked. It paid for itself but proved a poor investment for owners. The peak trading year for all three was 1839. There is a move to restore it.

London's Lost Route to the Sea P A L Vine David & Charles 1973 267pp

King Edwards School, Witley, originated in the same charter of Edward VI as St Thomas' Hospital and Christ's Hospital in 1553. It started in Bridewell Palace where Katherine of Aragon had lived and which the boy king gave the City of London at the suggestion of Bishop Ridley. The aim was to provide destitute youngsters with artisan skills, replacing the social services of the monasteries and chantries, recently dissolved. After a period in Southwark the school moved to new buildings in Witley in 1867. The buildings were requisitioned for the Royal Navy in WWII for the development of radar.

King Edwards School Bertie Mawer Ian Allan 2000 144pp

Ladywell Convent is the mother house of the Franciscan Missionaries of the Divine Motherhood, a nursing order. The house was built in 1911 as the family home of Major General Douglas Scott, Tuesley Court. It became Ladywell Convent in 1956, as HQ, international postulancy and novitiate, when many buildings were added and the nuns moved from their Guildford nursing home. The order de-centralised in 1979 and has branches in many countries.

Lammas Land was common land for growing hay but on which cattle could be grazed from Lammas, 1st August, to Candlemas, 2nd February.

Littleton was a Domesday Book manor, LITELTONE, held by Wulfwy Hunter before and after the conquest; presumably he was the king's hunter. Most of the old cottages in the village are 17th century: 8 & 9, 22 & 23, Pillar Box Cottage, Long Meadow, Littleton Farm & Willowmede.

Loseley House is open to visitors on summer afternoons. Loseley icecream used to be made here. Loseley was the Domesday Book LOSELE. The estate has been the home of the More (now More-Molyneux) family since the 16th century. Sir Christopher, Treasury Secretary to Henry VII bought the estate in 1508. His son, Sir William, an adviser to Elizabeth I, built the present house in the 1560s using Waverley Abbey stone after the dissolution. The muniment room yielded 2240 documents from Tudor times and earlier, letters, court rolls, etc. As the Mores were lords of other manors round about these are an important source for historians. Marrying the 17-year old Ann More in 1601 without her father's permission brought John Donne a year in prison which occasioned his epigram "John Donne, Ann Donne, undone"; to which we might add "well done" as they went on to produce at least 10 children!

Mare Hill Common was part of Witley Common but now belongs to Waverley BC. It is part of the heathland SSSI which stretches to Frensham. The abrupt transition from fields to heath corresponds to a fault which brings the more fertile Bargate beds up level with the less fertile sands above.

Milford Hospital pioneered tuberculosis treatment. It started as Surrey County Sanatorium in 1928. TB sufferers stayed three years or more to isolate them and give them the best living conditions to fight the bacterium. The 110 acres were worked by the patients for occupation, training and finance. After Thoracic Surgery moved to the Royal Surrey Hospital in Guildford it became a Rehabilitation Hospital for the Elderly in 1980.

The **Moat** pond is used for radio-controlled sailing dinghies, hence the buoys. It is absent from maps until the early OS editions so may have been dug in the mid 19th century, possibly as a duck pond.

Monks' Hatch, now the name of a house, would have been one of the ways to the farm when the Cistercians of Waverley Abbey owned Wanborough; its farmland stretched over the Hog's Back. The heavy-looking bargate bridge was by Lutyens for the Compton bypass of 1931, ornamented by crosses as it crosses the Pilgrim's Way. The new bridge for the A3 opened in 1989.

The **murdered sailor** was anonymous. Walking to Portsmouth he fell in with three travellers at Godalming. As they had no money he agreed to fund them on the journey. They were last seen together in the *Red Lion* at Thursley. The sailor's body was found at the spot now marked by a stone. The ruffians were arrested in Rake, trying to sell his belongings. Their bodies hung for some years on the gibbet. The sailor was buried at Thursley church. Baring Gould's Hardy-esque novel, *The Broom-squire*, tells of the life of the sailor's baby daughter in places around Thursley and the Devil's Punch Bowl.

The **North Downs Way** is a modern concoction for walkers designated in 1978 by the Countryside Commission. It runs 131 miles from Farnham to Dover mainly following ancient drove roads which are likely to be some of the oldest trade routes in England.

Oakhurst Cottage, Hambledon (National Trust 01428 684090) is open to the public some afternoons and can be visited by arrangement. It is a16th house, furnished as a 19th century labourer's dwelling.

Park House was built in the Italian style in the 1770's to the designs of Sir William Chambers. The 350 acre grounds were laid out by Capability Brown. The cedars in the fields are known to have been planted from pots in 1735. The cricket field was the scene of one of the earliest recorded cricket matches in 1727. The estate was home to the Brodrick family (the Viscounts Midleton) from 1713 until 1943 when two sons were killed in action. The house was used by the Canadian Army in WWII then became a special school and is now apartments. The finest building is the stable block, now a residence.

Peper Harow is an estate village with cottages, big house, church, farm and pond all in a cluster. Home Farm, Pevsner considers the best assemblage of farm buildings in Surrey, with its granary on wooden piers. The dovecote in the field was built in 1763; the dovecote at the farmyard entrance, in 1775. The church, St Nicholas, is first mentioned in a tax document of 1291. It is medieval in style but was rebuilt by Pugin in 1847. The tower had been added in 1826. Points of interest: the 1487 brass (near altar) for Joan Adderley; the memorial and grave of Sir Henry Dalrymple who led the charge of the Heavy Brigade at Balaclava; the stone about a stone in the chancel floor. The parish boundary appears in a charter of 909. The Domesday Book PIPERHERGE was a manor of 5 hides. There was an Anglo-Saxon personal name *Pippa* and *hearg* was a heathen temple.

The **Phillips Memorial** in Godalming was for Jack Phillips, the radio operator of the Titanic which sank in 1912. The cloisters were designed by Hugh Thackeray and the garden by Gertrude Jekyll.

The **pillboxes** are World War II relics of the GHQ line which stretched from the Medway to near Gloucester to defend London and the Midlands. The line follows natural obstacles such as the Downs, canals and rivers.

> *Pillboxes - a study of UK defences 1940* Henry Wills Secker & Warburg 1985 98pp

Polsted Manor was created by sub-division of the large Saxon manor of Compton before 1160. The present house is relatively modern. The gardener's cottage has Tudor features and may be part of the original manor house.

Postford and Waterloo Ponds appear in a map of 1660 and the lane runs along their dam which would have been built for the earliest gunpowder mills. Postford Mill (Albury Mill when demolished in 1996) was built in 1809 to make paper which it did until 1875. After this it made furniture fabric then animal feed. Finally it became a trout farm. Another Postford Mill, 100m upstream, owned by the same family was the one which made bank note paper execrated in Cobbett's *Rural Rides* He contrasted Chilworth's beauty with its industries: *two of the most damnable purposes namely the making of gunpowder and banknotes.* *Paper Mills of the Tillingbourne* A Crocker Tabard 1988 77pp

Prior's Field is an independent, trust school for 300 girls, 11-18. Founded by Julia Huxley, mother of Aldous, and grand daughter of Arnold of Rugby, the main building was by Charles Voysey of the Arts & Crafts Movement.

Puttenham village lies in an area with evidence of population from mesolithic times. The Domesday Book lists most villages round about but not Puttenham; it does state that Wanborough had formerly been two manors. The first documentary mention of Puttenham is from 1199. The medieval village had three fields under strip cultivation and the South Field probably gave its name to Suffield Lane. The Pilgrims' Way went through the village and there used to be a pilgrims' fair in December. The oldest houses are the 15th century timber-framed Rosemary Cottage, Old Cottage and Winter's Farm. The brick houses, Hook Lane Farm, Street Farm and Farm Cottage date from 1520-50.

> *Puttenham under the Hog's Back* Ruth Dugmore Phillimore 1987 247pp

Puttenham Church, St John The Baptist, is Norman in origin, the south wall of the nave dating from about 1100 and the pillars from about 1160. The tower was added about 1400 but lost its spire to fire in 1735. The window between the porch and the tower is the re-used early 14th century east window. There is a brass of 1481, a memorial for Edward Cranford, Rector. An ancient well in the churchyard came to light Palm Sunday 1972 when a tree disappeared!

Puttenham Common is worth exploring but very disorientating. It belongs to the Hampton Estate but is managed by SCC for recreation and conservation. An Iron Age fort, Hillbury, stands on the hilltop overlooking Hampton. Roman bricks and tiles have been found nearby and numerous Stone Age tools. Lascombe, at the eastern edge, is a Lutyens house.

Puttenham Priory is a 17th century brick house with a Palladian façade added by Thomas Park in the 18th century. It was never part of a monastery but the manor was willed to Newark Priory (near Woking) by Philippa de Melville in 1248. The priory would have drawn income from the profits of the land and an earlier manor house may have been occupied by its steward. In modern times the house has been a hospital and a business headquarters.

Rodsall Manor was probably the Domesday Book REDESSOLHAM, held in 1066 by the Saxon thegn, Tovi. In recent times a local historian has measured the field areas to show they accord with the Norman assessment of 5 hides. The present house was built in 1680 and two rooms were added in 1724.

St John's Seminary was built in 1890 for training priests for the Roman Catholic diocese of Southwark. It now acts as the regional seminary and takes overseas trainees. The red brick building is in the Jacobean Dutch style.

St Martha's Hill is a Greensand hill. The soft sands contain thin seams of sandstone which hold the hill together and form steps in the steep paths. Just south of the church a reservoir for Chilworth is sunk in the hill. Several round houses have been excavated here.

St Martha's Church is of Saxon origin but the oldest walls (the transepts) date from about 1087 and the chancel from about 1250. It was largely rebuilt in 1848. The hill seems to have been called Martyrs' Hill in Saxon times and the name may derive from this. During the 13th - 16th centuries the church was under Newark Abbey, the priest's house being below at Tyting Farm. By the east gate is a memorial stone to Yvonne Arnaud, the actress.

Shackleford was a tithing of Godalming. It has some of the best examples of bargate houses galetted with ironstone chips. The bargate Victorian Gothic church at Norney, St Mary, is by Sir Gilbert Scott in 13th century style.

Shalford was SHALDEFOR in the Domesday Book. One of the families to hold the estate in modern times was the Godwin-Austins of K2 fame. The Church, St Mary's, is Victorian but replaces an earlier building of 1789, and there were medieval and Saxon churches before that.

Shalford Mill on the Tilling Bourne still has its working parts intact and can be viewed 9.30am - 5pm. There was a mill on the site in 1332 but the present structure is 17th century. It was acquired for conservation by "Ferguson's Gang" in 1931 and now belongs to the National Trust.

Shamley Green is best seen when cricket is in progress; some of the roads are within the field of play and cottages have to be protected by nets. It appears in v5 of the Just So stories and somewhat earlier in a tax list of 1332 which had a Thomas ate Shamele, when it would have been a hamlet of Wonersh. Notables of the parish have been T S Eliot, W O Bentley (cars), Alfred Hitchcock and Harry Secombe. The church, Christ Church, was consecrated in 1864 as a chapel of Wonersh. The reredos and east wall are elaborately painted.

Shamley Green - a history of the village Shamley Green Hist Soc 1993 61pp

Snowdenham Hall was built in 1886 as a country mansion for Robert Courage the brewer. It is now apartments.

Somerset Bridge is a corruption of the name of an early ford, Sumeræs forda, listed in 909 as a boundary mark for Farnham in a charter of King Edgar.

Street House was the home of the London family that produced Sir Edwin Landseer Luytens, the architect, 1869-1944. His first job at 19 was to adapt the Thursley village shop and his early works were within reach of Thursley by bicycle. He completed 550 commissions: houses, memorials, cemeteries, palaces and bridges. The Surrey houses were succeeded by work all over the world: the British Embassy Washington, the Viceroy's residence New Delhi, the British Pavilion at the 1900 Paris Exhibition, the London Cenotaph.

Lutyens and the Edwardians Jane Brown Penguin 1997

Great Tangley Manor house is a fine moated Tudor house but only the roof and gables can be seen from the public paths. The timber framed front has the decorative curved braces, characteristic of eastern England and is dated 1582. The estate was cut off from the large manor of Bramley in the 13th century but acquired the name Great Tangley only in the 17th.

Thorncombe Street has the air of an ancient settlement. The name first appears in 1205 when Stephen de Turnham acquired the estate of Torncumba. Beatrice Lilley aka Lady Peel owned the estate in the 1930s.

Thursley lies on the old London-Portsmouth road. It is not in the Domesday Book, being then part of Witley Manor, but the Saxon church indicates there was already a settlement. It has several old and picturesque cottages near the church. Hill Farm, next to the churchyard, has soot on the rafters indicating the old part was a hall house, perhaps 14th century, and Wild Goose Cottage has a jutting upper storey unfashionable by 1550. See **Street House**.

Thursley Church, St Michael & All Angels, has a massive oak frame inserted around 1500 to support the bell turret. Points of interest: Saxon windows and wafer oven in the north wall of the chancel, a Saxon window in the nave; Saxon font; sundial on the tower; several 18th century table tombs; the graves of the murdered sailor (facing the war memorial) and John Freeman the poet.

Thursley Common is a National Nature Reserve of English Nature. It has the richest dragonfly fauna in Britain and all the British reptiles. Uncommon birds nest here: Dartford warbler, hobby, nightjar, stonechat, snipe, curlew and reed bunting. As well as dry heath there is raised bog with the irregular holes of old peat diggings. The Cricklestone and Thor's Stone are ancient boundary marks, Thor's probably aquiring its romantic name from *The Broom-squire*. The long mound with the board walks is on the Saxon boundary of AD 688, when the Wessex king, Cædwalla, gave the Farnham lands to the Bishop of Winchester.

The **Tilling Bourne** is a major tributary of the River Wey. It runs for about 20 km/13 miles parallel with the chalk and Greensand ridges fed by springs from both and joins the Wey at Shalford waterworks. It powered up to

30 mills and was a major industrial valley in Britain from medieval times until coal based industry started. It now has trout farms and watercress beds.

Tuesley was TIWESLE in the Domesday Book. Tiw was a Saxon god. This area has a great concentration of pre-Christian Saxon names in England (Wanborough, Thursley, Peper Harow, etc). The first influx of Saxons seems to have come across the Weald from the coast of Kent and Sussex and according to Bede the Kingdom of Sussex was the last to be Christianised.

Tuesley Minster is thought to be the 2nd church listed in the Domesday Book entry for Godalming and is probably 7th century. It existed long before the parish system and would have been the religious centre for the whole district. Excavated in 1860, the building had a nave of 21' x 14' and a room with nine skeletons. Pope Gregory advised St Augustine to put churches on the sites of existing temples, so it is likely that Tiw was worshipped here.

Unsted Park is a rehabilitation hospital. The Adam-style house was built in 1750 by John Sparkes and the stables were added in 1874. It was a hospital in WW I and a training centre for the National Provincial Bank 1949-72.

Unsted Manor is an attractive half-timbered house just off the route, built in the 14th & 16th centuries but not a true manor house. The name first appears in a document in 1256 as Tunchamstede.

Unsted Bridge is the lowest of the 13th century bridges attributed to the monks of Waverley, like those at Eashing and Tilford. It crosses only a backwater now, the River Wey having moved across the valley.

Wanborough was the Saxon manor WENEBERGE of the Domesday Book. Its Lord, Leofwin, according to tradition, was killed at the battle of Hastings. A few days later it was laid waste by the Norman army skirting London prior to the English capitulation. It was bought for £100 in 1130 as a grange for the new Waverley Abbey whose lay-brothers would have worked it, hence the local place names with *monk* or *greyfriars*. It gave its name to Wanborough Illinois when Morris Birkbeck, the tenant farmer emigrated to America in 1817 with workers from Wanborough and Puttenham. St Bartholomew's was a Saxon church re-built in the 12th century with defensive strength.

Wanborough from White Barrow to World War Gillian Drew 1993 28pp

Wanborough Manor house was the farm house of the one-farm manor. It bears the date 1527 when it still belonged to Waverley Abbey but architectural detail suggests it was built 1650-70. In World War II it was the SOE (Special Operations Executive) training centre for resistance organisers for France and it flits through the espionage novels of Ted Allbeury. Trainees were not allowed to speak English and local people called them the foreigners.

Wanborough Great Barn is Surrey's most important medieval aisled barn. Guildford Museum arranges open days and group visits. 1388 is the building date suggested by tree ring data but the octagonal pillars were cut early in that century, presumably for an earlier building. The barn was in agricultural use until about 1988 and was fully restored in 1997. It was not a tithe barn.

Watts Chapel in the cemetery is extraordinary. Financed by Watts and designed by his wife Mary (d 1938) it is in Italian Romanesque style with symbolism based on the Circle of Eternity and the Cross of Faith. The bricks and decorative gesso panels were made at the terracotta works by 74 villagers.

The Word in the Pattern Mrs Watts Astolat 1904 / *Watts Chapel* Veronica Franklyn Gould

Watts Gallery is free and open most afternoons. It displays 500 works of the painter and sculptor George Watts. Art treasures from the London galleries were stored here in WWII. The adjacent buildings were a studio and factory for terracotta ware until 1956 using the underlying Gault clay. The 1950's TV potter's wheel interlude was filmed here. A Roman house excavated in 1914 in the Watts' garden at the nearby Limnerlease yielded three coins dated from 313 to 378. George Frederick Watts (1817-1904) sold 5 shilling portraits at the age of 16 and served as the House Artist to the British Ambassador in Florence. His best known bronze is *Physical Energy* in Kensington Gardens. He was a friend of Dickens, Thackeray and Tennyson. His first wife was Ellen Terry.

Westbrook House in Godalming is a Jacobean house with Georgian additions owned by *The Meath*, a charitable home and centre for epileptics. General James Oglethorpe (1696-1785), inherited it and lived there. He was an MP for Haslemere, a general of ambivalent affinities in the army that put down the Jacobite rebellion and the founder of the American colony of Georgia (1732).

Westbrook Mill is probably on the site of one of the Domesday Book mills. Westbrokesmyll appears in the leet records of 1483. In 1881when it was a leather works it generated for the first electric town lighting anywhere.

The Brilliant Ray Francis Haverton Godalming Centenary Celebration Committee 1981 18pp

The **wetlands** near Unsted are watermeadows of the Wey which have snipe, teal, shoveller ducks, dab chicks and water rails, easy to see in winter.

Winkworth Arboretum (National Trust) is open dawn to dusk all the year. It started as a private venture. Wilfred Fox (1875-1962) a London doctor living nearby bought 95 acres in 1937 which he cleared and planted with temperate, broad leaved exotics, maples, Azaleas, Liquidambars and Sorbus species. He gave a 62 acre site to the NT in 1952 and 35 acres more in 1957.

Wintershall was an estate cut off from the great Manor of Bramley around 1227. In 1723 it was bought by the Barretts (of Wimpole Street). In recent years it has been the venue for a summer passion play.

Witley was the large Domesday Book manor WITLEI with nothing else listed before the Sussex border. It was rated for 20 hides and it had a church. The malmsied Duke of Clarence was one of its medieval owners. Ancient variants of the name rarely have *h* so the likely derivation is *Witta's* not *white clearing*. George Eliot (née Mary Ann Evans 1819-1880) lived at Witley Heights from 1876 until shortly before she died; she wrote her last novel, *Threophrastus Such*, here. Witley Station is on the London - Portsmouth main line (1849). The waste of the ancient manor became Hindhead, Thursley and Witley Commons.

The History of Witley, Milford and the surrounding area Elizabeth Forster 1999 Witley P C 83pp

Witley Church, All Saints, has a Norman doorway inside the Victorian porch but most of the nave wall is late Saxon, 1½ windows surviving from that time The wall paintings are 12th century. The style of the chancel, transepts and tower is Early English and a 12th century roof survives in the south transept. Like most ancient churches the windows have been enlarged in later styles.

Witley Park is now a conference centre with very fine gardens. It used to be Lea Park. In modern times it has been owned by a succession of industrialists but was emparked in the original sense for deer hunting in 1247. The 3-mile Bargate wall was built in the 1890s. Lord Pirrie, a Belfast ship builder, owner in the 1900s, was the cause of P in the old iron gates of the estate.

Wonersh has splendid old houses suggesting ancient settlement. It is not in the Domesday Book, however, probably then being part of the large manor of Bramley. The Pepper Pot in the road junction is a village folly originally conceived as a bus shelter. On the green is a Victorian reading room built for the Gosden tannery workers. The *Grantley Arms* is a genuine old house with olde worlde additions. It was the *Hector Inn* in 1687. It was used in the first Dick Turpin (silent) film in 1912. *Woodyers* is a 17th century house improved in the 18th. *Green Place* is a Georgian house with a 16th century wing and has internal work back to the 14th century. The jettied, timber framed *Old House* in the main street dates from about 1600; the middle section was jacked to a higher level in 1979 to prevent flooding. In the gate house to the field beside the churchyard see the high frieze in low relief modelled on villagers in 1953. The church, St John the Baptist, is largely 18th & 19th century but the oldest fabric may be part of one of the DB churches of Bramley. Points of interest: the arch between the tower and nave of around 1180; several brasses.

Wonersh - a Guide to its Principal Buildings Wonersh History Society 1996 44pp

Wonersh Mill is now a store shed on the other side of the mill pond from the house. A map of 1679 shows a corn mill here. The mill house dates from the 15th century but has had many additions.. Milling ceased in 1910.

Wormley has no records ancient enough to allow interpretation of its name but *snake clearing* would seem appropriate. It is a hamlet of Witley enlarged by Coopers' factory which made walking sticks from coppiced wood and the school, **King Edward's**. The wartime Naval presence led to the establishment of the Institute of Oceanographic Sciences in 1952 which developed sonar for the mapping of the oceans but moved to Southampton in 1995.

The **Wyatt Almshouses** were built about 1622 funded by £500 in the will of Richard Wyatt, 1554-1619, who lived at Hall Place in Shackleford (now gone). He owned the Dunsfold foundry and had other irons in the fire, eg a wharf in London. He was elected Master of the Carpenters' Company of London.

Yagden Hill, 83m/272 feet, has a gravel cap which was the river bed of the proto-Blackwater or its tributaries in the Ice Age when glacial outwash brought stones from further south. This river system was captured by the Wey and the remaining puny Blackwater now starts at Aldershot.